EFFECTING ORGANIZATIONAL RENEWAL IN SCHOOLS:
A SOCIAL SYSTEMS PERSPECTIVE

Edmund Short

EDUCATIONAL LEADERSHIP LIBRARY
SCHOOL MANAGEMENT INSTITUTE
Located on the
University of South Florida Campus
and funded by

|I|D|E|A| REPORTS ON SCHOOLING
JOHN I. GOODLAD, *General Editor and Director*

EARLY SCHOOLING SERIES
Assisted by Jerrold M. Novotney

SERIES ON EDUCATIONAL CHANGE
Assisted by Kenneth A. Tye

EFFECTING ORGANIZATIONAL RENEWAL IN SCHOOLS: A SOCIAL SYSTEMS PERSPECTIVE

Richard C. Williams
Charles C. Wall
W. Michael Martin
Arthur Berchin

Foreword by
Samuel G. Sava
Executive Director |I|D|E|A|

Introduction by
J. W. Getzels
University of Chicago

A CHARLES F. KETTERING FOUNDATION PROGRAM

McGRAW-HILL BOOK COMPANY
New York   St. Louis   San Francisco   Düsseldorf
London   Mexico   Sydney   Toronto

Library of Congress Cataloging in Publication Data
Main entry under title:

Effecting organizational renewal in schools.

(|I|D|E|A| reports on schooling. Series on educational change)
    Includes bibliographical references.
    1. School management and organization—Addresses, essays, lectures. 2. Educational sociology—Addresses, essays, lectures. I. Williams, Richard C. II. Series: Institute for Development of Educational Activities. Series on educational change.
LB2806.E43   371.2   73-17162
ISBN 0-07-070408-2

ACKNOWLEDGMENTS

Acknowledgments for permission to reprint selections from copyrighted material are as follows:

J. W. Getzels, "The Conflicts and Role Behavior in the Educational Setting," in W. W. Charters, Jr., and N. L. Gage, eds., *Readings in the Social Psychology of Education.* Copyright 1963 by Allyn and Bacon, Inc. Used by permission of the publisher.

George D. Spindler, "Education in a Transforming American Culture," *Harvard Educational Review.* Copyright 1955 by the President and Fellows of Harvard College. Used by permission of the publisher.

|I|D|E|A| is the service mark for the Institute for Development of Educational Activities, Inc., an incorporated affiliate of the Charles F. Kettering Foundation.

|I|D|E|A| was established in 1965 to encourage constructive change in elementary and secondary schools. It serves as the primary operant for the Foundation's missions and programs in education.

As an institution committed to stimulating constructive changes for the benefit of mankind, the Kettering Foundation believes strongly in the potential of education to help bring about such changes.

Robert G. Chollar

President and
Chief Executive Officer
Charles F. Kettering Foundation

CONTENTS

E. Short

04/74

FOREWORD

This volume is part of a series pertaining to educational change and school improvement, developed out of research conducted by the Research Division of the Institute for Development of Educational Activities, Inc. (|I|D|E|A|). |I|D|E|A| was established by the Charles F. Kettering Foundation in 1965 as its educational affiliate and given the specific mission of accelerating the pace of change in education. Before advocating yet another collection of "innovations" based on the insights then available, we decided to begin by examining the total context in which change was to take place. Under the direction of Dr. John I. Goodlad, |I|D|E|A|'s Research Division formed eighteen schools from eighteen Southern California districts into the "League of Cooperating Schools" to participate in the design and testing of a new strategy for educational improvement. Several volumes in the series now being published by McGraw-Hill report on the variety of human and organizational influences that operated within this new social system of schools.

It would be both premature and pointless to highlight here the basic findings of this study. Each finding must be put in context before its significance can be appreciated. Suffice it to say that, while a school complex must have the desire to change before it can do so, desire is not enough—all seeking to improve it must also understand what Dr. Goodlad calls "the ecology of change," the complex of factors that can defeat the most conscientious efforts to improve.

The volume you are about to read does not, however, report directly on the strategies and findings regarding educational change pertaining to the "League" model for school improvement. Rather, it deals with the larger, theoretical context of institutional renewal in general and summarizes several empirical studies conducted within this theoretical frame. All of these studies were made possible by the Research Division of |I|D|E|A| and, taken as a composite whole, contribute significantly to the principles and concepts developed through the encompassing, larger study.

We are pleased that Professor J. W. Getzels, to whom we are indebted for his insightful Introduction, sees this volume as serving to support his own seminal work on psychosociological approaches to the understanding of organizations and institutions. Much of what follows will be of interest to researchers and theoreticians. However, the authors have endeavored to present their material so as to attract, also, the attention of thoughtful practitioners interested in understanding and effecting change in the educational organizations in which they work.

The Study of Educational Change and School Improvement provided much of the strategy for the |I|D|E|A| Change Program for Individually Guided Education (IGE) now being used in several hundred schools. It spawned studies such as those reported here. And it supported in one way or another the related work of nearly forty candidates for doctoral degrees. On behalf of |I|D|E|A| and the Charles F. Kettering Foundation, I wish to express gratitude to the school board members, administrators, teachers, children, and parents who made all this possible.

Samuel G. Sava
Executive Director
|I|D|E|A|

INTRODUCTION

Research on the organization and administration of schools has moved through a number of phases: from the use of simple variables to the use of complex variables, from descriptive studies to experimental studies, from theoretical models of the school as a technical system to theoretical models of the school as a social system. These phases were not saccadic; they flowed into each other imperceptibly. Nonetheless, I myself can remember when a suggestion that the school might be studied in theoretical as well as descriptive terms was dismissed contemptuously by a leading education journal as "up in Cloud 17." Theoretical studies might be useful elsewhere, but in education they were "merely theoretical."

The theoretical model on which the present study is founded was foreshadowed in the 1952 article "A Psycho-Sociological Framework for the Study of Educational Administration," which acknowledged its debt to the work of Talcott Parsons.[1] During the ensuing years, the model underwent a number of elaborations and refinements. Crucial in these developments were the collaboration of Egon Guba and the critical study devoted to the model in a dozen or more empirical dissertations by several cohorts of brilliant students in the Department of Education at Chicago. In due course the interdisciplinary model was hardly recognizable from its initial formulation and included the following elements: a psychological element represented by the central concept of *personal disposition,* a sociological element represented by the central concept of *role expectation,* and an anthropological element represented by the central concept of *cultural value,* all embedded in a particular *environment.* Behavior in the school as a social

[1] J. W. Getzels, "A Psycho-Sociological Framework for the Study of Educational Administration," *Harvard Educational Review,* vol. 22, no. 4, 1952, pp. 235–246.

system was seen as emerging from the interaction of these personal, institutional, cultural, and environmental forces.

This is not the place to review the numerous conceptual and empirical issues derived from the model and applied to research and practice; a sampling is given in the treatise *Educational Administration as a Social Process: Theory, Research, Practice.*[2] But there seems hardly any doubt that for better or worse—and probably for a little of each—the model has had an impact on both educational research and practice. It has given rise to a multitude of empirical studies (the authors of the present volume state that some hundred items have been located); it has found its way into numerous textbooks not only in administration but in other aspects of education as well; and, most surprising in view of the abstract nature of the formulation, it has influenced a half-dozen projects in the United States, England, and Australia attempting to reconstitute the training of school personnel. The proposal for the prototypical project—the Ford Training and Placement Project at the University of Chicago already in operation for five years—is given in "Education for the Inner City: A Practical Proposal by an Impractical Theorist."[3]

The most recent elaboration of the model and its application to research and practice may be found in the chapter "A Social Psychology of Education" in the *Handbook of Social Psychology,*[4] which represents a rather interesting reversal of what is said to be the customary movement of ideas and models. Usually ideas and models are said to move from the basic discipline to the applied field; in this case, the ideas and model seem to have moved at least as much from the applied field to the basic discipline. It seems to me that the familiar dichotomies like basic research versus applied research, pure ideas versus practical ideas, academic theory versus common sense create more mischief than they are worth; I know of no practical problem that is not related to some conceptual issue, and no conceptual issue which may not be related sooner or later to a practical problem.

As James Bryant Conant put it, "Literally, every step we take in life is determined by a series of interlocking concepts and conceptual

[2] Jacob W. Getzels, James M. Lipham, and Roald F. Campbell, *Educational Administration as a Social Process,* Harper and Row, New York, 1968.
[3] J. W. Getzels, "Education for the Inner City: A Practical Proposal by an Impractical Theorist," *School Review,* vol. 75, no. 3, Autumn 1967, pp. 283–299.
[4] J. W. Getzels, "A Social Psychology of Education," in Gardner Lindzey and Elliot Aronson (eds.), *Handbook of Social Psychology,* 2nd ed., Addison, Wesley, Reading, Mass., 1969, vol. v, chap. 42, pp. 459–537.

schemes. Every goal we formulate for our actions, every decision we make, be it trivial or momentous, involves assumptions about the universe and about human beings. To my mind, any attempt to draw a sharp line between common-sense ideas and scientific concepts is not only impossible but unwise."[5] I would only add to this that the difference between common-sense ideas and scientific concepts is that in the former the underlying assumptions and theoretical views are implicit and may remain private, for the latter the underlying assumptions and theoretical view are explicit and must be made public.

The present volume reports a research study of organizational renewal in eight elementary schools. The inquiry founded explicitly in the model of a school as a social system speaks at once both to conceptual issues and practical problems. All eight schools had undertaken to achieve change. Four ranked high in organizational renewal, and four ranked low. What, the authors asked, are the systematic organizational and administrative concomitants of the ability to attain the desired goal?

More specifically, the authors posed three questions in the terms given by the model. The first question was: What is the relationship between the way the principal was perceived by the teachers and the school's organizational renewal ranking? A significant relation was found between the teachers' perceptions of the principal as more concerned with their personal dispositions than with the role expectations of the institution and the ability to achieve organizational change.

By the very nature of things, however, the dispositions of the individual and the expectations of the institution are bound to be incompatible in some degree. Short of utopia, the organizational situation inevitably entails certain types of strain or conflict demanding adaptation by the individual, adjustment by the institution, or some combination of the two. Hence the second question: What is the relation of types of strain or conflict between personal dispositions and role expectations, modes of adaptation to the strain or conflict, and ability to achieve organizational renewal? Significant relations were found between types of strain or conflict, modes of adaptation, and the degree of organizational renewal found in the school.

Although there have been previous studies relating leadership and conflict in the educational setting, I know of no other study relating leadership, conflict, and modes of adaptation. Taken together these

[5] James B. Conant, *Modern Science and Modern Man*, Doubleday, New York, 1953, pp. 135–136.

investigations are a contribution of theoretical, empirical, and practical import.

But the school cannot be understood without relation to the culture of which it is a part. The values prevailing in the school must be placed in the context of the values of the culture in which the school is located. This led to the third question: Are the relationships among the values of the teachers, the principals, and the parents associated with the school's organizational renewal ranking?

I shall not give away the results—I have perhaps already done too much of that—except to say that they raise issues of the utmost interest regarding the values of teachers, principals, and parents, and illustrate the uses of working within an explicit theoretical model. Previous work in the same conceptual terms in the middle fifties had shown systematic relationships between traditional and emergent values for several age and school groups. A number of these relationships were not observed in the present study and, if I may refer to some recent work of my own, I too found differences in this domain between the observations in the middle fifties and in the late sixties.[6] When the previous studies and the present ones are examined together, one is faced with the question whether there may not have been a shift in values during the turbulent sixties which may account for the discrepant results. My point here is not that such shift actually occurred, although I believe that at least in part it did, and it is not to speak favorably of the specific model underlying the present study. My point rather is that insofar as the work is placed in an explicit model, the results of the studies done within its terms shed light on one another. The whole becomes greater than the sum of the separate parts. And more, the results of past and present studies not only illuminate each other but raise fruitful issues and give direction to future studies.

In an integrative last chapter where the overall quantitative data are combined with case studies of the individual schools, the authors relate their results to the general program of organizational renewal. They rightly say that there is no question as to the need for change in the structure of American schools. The reason "change agents" and such have not been successful in effecting long-range change is not that what they were trying to accomplish was of little utility but that they underestimated the complexity of the school as a social system—

[6] J. W. Getzels, "On the Transformation in Values: A Decade after Port Huron," *School Review*, vol. 80, no. 4, August 1972, pp. 505–519.

a complexity the present research makes eminently clear—and the complexity of change itself.

As I have argued in greater detail elsewhere, change is not monolithic; there are several types of change that must be distinguished if the difficulties of introducing change and the resistance to accepting change are to be understood.[7] One type of change is *enforced change*, i.e., alterations that are imposed upon the school by pressures from outside the school. This type of change often gives rise within the school to resistance and counterpressures resulting in *expedient change*, i.e., alterations that are devised by the school for the paradoxical reason of avoiding true change. Put another way, it is an accommodation by the school to maintain its existing system rather than transform it in principle. There is a third type of change, which may be called *essential change*, i.e., transformations that are neither merely an accommodation to external pressure or a tactic for resisting transformation but that spring from the needs, initiative, and imagination of the individuals within the school although the stimulus may, of course, come from outside. It is this type of voluntaristic change that makes for genuine renewal within the school. But insofar as a modification of the school has effects on the culture within which the school is embedded, from the external point of view there is then a fourth type of change—*extruded change*, i.e., transformations in the school which entail modification in related systems such as the family or the community. The extruded change may be seen by these related systems as enforced upon them and give rise to outright resistance (as in the case of busing) or to mere expedient change (tokenism) frustrating essential change in the school quite as the school often frustrates change that is enforced upon it. The administrator must be aware of these types of change and the difficulties each involves if he is to effect renewal.

This volume may be read with profit by theorists, researchers, academics, and administrators. The theorist will recognize shortcomings in the model and may want to modify it in the light of the empirical data; it is, for example, clear that the model omits political, economic, and, perhaps most importantly, historical variables. The researcher will find a plenitude of issues to investigate in greater detail, an obvious instance being the relation between types of conflict in the

[7] J. W. Getzels, "Creative Administration and Organizational Change: An Essay in Theory," in L. J. Rubin (ed.), *Frontiers in School Leadership*, Rand McNally, Chicago, 1970, pp. 69–85.

educational setting and modes of individual adaptation to the conflict —a subject opened up by the present study. The academic may be stimulated to consider whether he ought not to encourage more cooperative doctoral research instead of the present fragmentary dissertations. The school administrator will not only find much to ponder in the abstract issues but will be able to compare his own situation with the conditions described in the case studies of these schools attempting to achieve renewal: What, for example, are the teacher's perceptions of his leadership compared to those of the schools under study? What are the characteristic modes of adaptation to stress in his school? What is the relation between the values prevailing in his school and the values of the community which it presumably serves?

The work bears witness to the proposition that theory and theory-based inquiry in education are not necessarily "up in Cloud 17," as was charged not too long ago, and that John Dewey's well-known but often neglected dictum is well worth heeding: "Theory is in the end ... the most practical of all things, because the widening of the range of attention beyond nearby purpose and desire eventually results in the creation of wider and further-reaching purposes and enables us to make use of a much wider and deeper range of conditions and means than were expressed in the observation of primitive practical purposes."[8]

J. W. Getzels
R. Wendell Harrison Distinguished Service Professor
in the Departments of Education and of Psychology,
The University of Chicago
July 9, 1973

---

[8] John Dewey, *Sources of a Science of Education*, Liveright, New York, 1929, p. 17.

ACKNOWLEDGMENTS

This volume is divided into three separate but interrelated parts. Charles C. Wall examined the leader behavior dimension (reported here in Chapter 2), W. Michael Martin examined the role–personality conflict and adaptation dimension (Chapter 3), and Arthur Berchin examined the value dimension (Chapter 4). Chapter 5, which attempts to synthesize the implications of the data reported here, was prepared by Richard C. Williams. The introductory Chapter 1 was prepared jointly by the authors.

In a very real sense, this was a joint project with each participant contributing fully, though in different ways, to the final report. Drs. Wall, Martin, and Berchin shared the data-collecting chores and assumed the major burden of the data analysis. Professor Williams supervised the project and reviewed the manuscripts. Charles Wall supervised the rewriting of the initial studies for publication purposes with the editorial assistance of Judith S. Golub.

We are indebted to many who helped us, particularly to Professor J. W. Getzels of the University of Chicago, whose model provides the rationale for our examination of elementary schools and who visited with us early in the development of the project and helped us to clarify our thinking and focus our efforts. In addition, he was kind enough to review our papers and serve as a respondent when we originally reported our research at an AERA Symposium in New York City in February 1971. Professor James Lipham of the University of Wisconsin also was kind enough to review our papers and serve as a respondent at the New York seminar. Professor Philip J. Runkel of the Center for Advanced Study of Educational Administration, Eugene, Oregon, offered helpful advice during the early stages of the project. Professors William McKelvey, Robert Pace, Hans Schollhammer, Jay D. Scribner,

Gerald Slayton, and Michael Yashino served on a joint doctoral examining committee and offered many constructive suggestions on the study.

We owe a special debt of gratitude to the many staff members of the Research Division of the Institute for Development of Educational Activities, Inc., under the direction of John I. Goodlad. Mary M. Bentzen, Ann Lieberman, Sol Roshal, Alice Z. Seeman, and Kenneth A. Tye were very generous in sharing their research findings with us and in critiquing our studies. Bette Overman spent many hours preparing the statistical treatments and devising computer programs for the entire study. In addition, she provided considerable assistance in preparing the manuscripts for publication.

We express our greatest gratitude to the educators who participated in this study. To the eight principals who were sufficiently self-confident and willing to take the risk of allowing us into their schools, we extend our sincere thanks and admiration. We thank also the teachers who patiently completed our instruments and so candidly answered our questions.

CHAPTER 1
STUDYING SCHOOLS
AS SOCIAL SYSTEMS

It has become almost a cliché to lament the ineffectiveness of America's public schools. We are all familiar with the vast literature that has accumulated about the public schools' shortcomings: the schools do not teach fundamental skills; their curriculum is not relevant to the times; they are rigid and closed; they employ inadequately trained teachers; they are not sufficiently businesslike in their management; and, to add the newest all-encompassing concept, they lack "accountability." Similarly, the public is familiar with at least some of the many remedies and nostrums that have been proposed to set the schools right: more money, better curriculum, improved teacher and administrator training programs, use of PPBS (planning-programming-budgeting systems), and more effective teacher negotiations.

Accompanying these various prescriptions and allegedly supporting them has been a vast amount of educational research. This research activity has covered a wide range of topics, and, like research in most fields of inquiry, it has been compiled, annotated, summarized, and synthesized. Unfortunately, the enormous writing, prescribing, and research in education have had little effect on what goes on in the schools. As Sarason, picking up an old theme, has stated, "The more things change, the more they remain the same."[1]

As an example of this problem, it is instructive to look at school leadership. A common observation made about schools by parents, teachers, and scholars alike is that they suffer from poor administrative leadership. Indeed, a rallying point in the teacher negotiations movement has been to overcome the intolerable burden of inept leadership that has, in their opinion, limited their opportunities to teach effectively.

A variety of corrective measures has been suggested, ranging from designing more effective administrator training programs, mandating the use of various technical tools in school management (management by objectives or PPBS), or diminishing the administrator's role through increased participation in decision-making by parents and teachers.

In addition, there has been considerable research literature on leadership that has developed in education and elsewhere. Both the traitist and situationist approaches have been rather thoroughly explored, and such explorations have been summarized and synthesized by several scholars.[2] However, the findings from all this research on leadership have been quite contradictory, and few generalizations can be made that have consistent implications for the training of administrators or for improving administrative behavior in the schools. As a result, all of the research, speculations, and prescriptions appear to have had a very limited impact on administrative leadership in the public schools.

Purpose of the Study

It is apparent in an era of change that schools must have some way to respond to the variety of alternatives available to them. It is our observation that some schools are able to adapt themselves to the pressures of change, to set goals for themselves and achieve them. Others in the same situation flounder. What is it that determines whether a school will be able to achieve its stated goals? We have labeled the process by which they do so *organizational renewal* and have attempted to study and define this process and to relate it to various factors in the school's social system.

The three interrelated studies reported here represent an attempt at a systematic inquiry into the reasons for a school's ability to attain its goals. The particular focus of the research was the relationship between selected dimensions of the school's social system and the school's ability to effect organizational renewal. The project was designed so that a comprehensive picture of this relationship might emerge. We expected that this approach would address some of the limitations we felt plagued many of the research studies we had examined. Some of these limitations were:

Unidimensionality Schools are complex organizations, yet much of the research to date has been an attempt to look at how some isolated factor or dimension found in schools is related to organization functioning. Thus, to follow up on the leadership example, a researcher might determine some one measure of successful leadership and look for concomitant variations associated with measured effective or ineffective leadership. It is not surprising that such one-dimensional efforts have been unproductive. Leadership is but one factor in a complex environment embedded in a broad social framework. No real understanding of leadership can be gained unless it is viewed as a part of this broader context.

Superficiality Related to the foregoing discussion is the surprising degree to which the historical framework within which a school exists is ignored in educational research. Most research is based on data obtained at a given point in time. The effect of events leading up to or surrounding the data collection often is not considered. For example, any assessment of the leader behavior of an administrator must take into account the length of time he has been in that school and the history of recent pressures that have been exerted on the school by influential agents (school board, citizens, teachers, pupils). These factors may influence, and indeed shape, a leader's behavior.

Homeostasis The dynamic relationship among teachers, students, administrators, and the public is often neglected. The fact that various conditions exist alongside each other may be acknowledged, but the dynamic interplay of these factors is often left unexamined by a sustained research thrust. For example, it may be unfair to lament the seemingly authoritarian administrative practices of some inner-city school administrators without considering the harsh, perplexing, and sometimes hostile environment within which many such administrators must work, caused by such factors as high pupil and teacher turnover, diverse community attitudes or activities, and high absenteeism. The understandably authoritarian administrative leadership style may, in turn, decrease pupil and teacher morale and heighten the turnover problems. Thus, any realistic examination of, say, the problems of inner-city schools must seek to encompass this complex dynamic interplay among persons, positions, and events. Not to do so is to ignore the reality of schools as complex organizations.

But how does one go about identifying these many components, much less examining several of them at the same time and predicting the dynamic relationship among them? This is the value of theory. It provides one with a framework from which these components can be identified and examined and upon which predictions can be made.

While much research, as we have indicated, has been based on some theoretical formulation, all too many research studies have identified a single concept or variable and examined it to see if it responded to theoretical expectations. This examination of singular dimensions of dynamic theoretical formulations is almost a self-contradictory exercise because the research attempts a static explanation of a dynamic process. Thus, the purpose of this research study was to conduct a multidimensional examination of the social structure of elementary schools. We had two primary goals in conducting this inquiry:

1. To gain further insights into selected dimensions of the social systems of schools and to examine the way in which these components interact to form a dynamic system; and

2. To examine the relationship between the characteristics of a school's social system and the school's ability to achieve organizational renewal.

Theoretical Framework

J. W. Getzels and his associates at the University of Chicago developed a theoretical model for analyzing behavior in a social system. Because of the variables to be investigated in this study, the Getzels–Guba Model[3] was deemed most appropriate for our purposes.

Three classes of phenomena may be observed in the illustration of the Getzels model: (1) the nomothetic or normative, which includes the roles and expectations which will fulfill the goals of the system; (2) the idiographic or personal, which includes the personalities and need-dispositions of the individual within the institution; and (3) the cultural, which includes the ethos and values of the individuals, the institution, and the institution's environment.

This model was first advanced by Getzels and draws heavily upon the work of Barnard, Lewin, Riesman, Parsons, Bakke, and Argyris.[4] Several studies have indicated that the Getzels model represents a useful framework within which to conduct research.[5] In addition, over one hundred studies have employed the concepts and dimensions of the model in conducting research.[6]

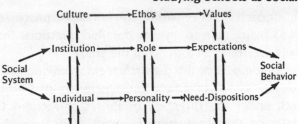

FIGURE 1.1 OPERATIONAL MODEL OF MAJOR DIMENSIONS OF SOCIAL BEHAVIOR

From J. W. Getzels, "Conflict and Role Behavior in the Educational Setting," in W. W. Charters, Jr., and N. L. Gage (eds.), *Readings in the Social Psychology of Education.* Copyright 1963 by Allyn and Bacon, Inc. Reprinted by permission of the publisher.

Research Team

Exploring the various dimensions of a social system can be a complex task, with one individual unable to expend the necessary time or financial resources requisite to conducting such an in-depth analysis. For this reason, three researchers with mutual interests came together to dissect the model into three parts based upon the perspectives developed above: people, processes, and concepts. Thus, the three parts to the theoretical model—leader behavior, values, and role conflict and adaptation—could be examined in detail and later fitted back together for purposes of generalizing the applicability of the model to social science research. In retrospect, the team approach proved to be an extremely valuable research tool. The researchers were able to explore common problems and critically analyze each other's research techniques, scoring procedures, conclusions, and recommendations. The team approach also made possible the sharing of field data collection activities and thus expanded considerably the number of teachers and principals interviewed at length in a very short time. The background of the researchers was also diverse. One came from the field of business administration, another from English, while the third had experience in educational administration. Thus, the interactions of the group had an interdisciplinary flavor.

Prior to actual data collection, common procedures were developed which would minimize the overlap, yet maximize the amount of data to be collected. Through dialogue and collaboration covering every aspect of the three studies, the research team was able to obtain information for each other regarding the concepts, processes, and people, as well as being able to answer detailed questions from teachers and principals regarding all aspects of the study.

The three members of the research team were doctoral candidates at the Graduate School of Education, University of California at Los Angeles, and, under the direction of Professor Richard C. Williams, worked jointly on the study from February 1969 through May 1970. It would be difficult to separate individual from group contributions, since the procedures and methods described below were the product of the team's consensus decision making, imagination, and labor, along with the stimulation provided by the members of the Research Division at |I|D|E|A|. The leadership component was the responsibility of Charles C. Wall,[7] while W. Michael Martin studied conflict and adaptation.[8] Arthur Berchin sought to identify the effects of values upon the functioning of the school as a social system,[9] and it was the responsibility of Richard C. Williams to attempt a synthesis of the three perspectives. In addition, J. W. Getzels, University of Chicago, and Philip J. Runkel, Center for the Advanced Study of Educational Administration, Eugene, Oregon, provided the research team with extremely valuable insights and dialogue relative to conducting such a study.

Variables Being Measured

Three components of the Getzels model were found appropriate for an examination of the elementary school as a social system. The variables we selected were: (1) leader behavior; (2) teacher role–personality conflict and adaptation; and (3) value orientations of both the school's personnel and its immediate community. The leadership component involves the interaction between the institution and the individual working within that institution. As illustrated by the Getzels model, the institution's formal representative, identified in a school as a principal, helps determine the roles which need to be filled and interprets the expectations the institution has for individuals occupying those roles. In turn, the individuals who occupy these roles have certain personalities and need-dispositions that must be satisfied. It is the blending of the need-dispositions of the individual and the expectations of the institution which allow any organization to function as a viable social system.

Since teachers may perceive their roles differently depending on their own individual personality and need-dispositions, it is important to the understanding of the school as a social system to identify their methods of adaptation to those differences in role expectations. The method of adaptation may well be indicative of the school's ability to function as a cohesive unit.

Underlying the role expectations of the institution and the need-dispositions of the individuals within the institution are value orientations. It was hoped that identifying the value orientations of both the principal and teachers of an elementary school would lead to a more thorough understanding of the institution's role expectations and the individual's need-dispositions. In addition to identifying the value orientation within the institution, it is important to assess the values held by those in the community surrounding the school.

It is these three variables identified from the Getzels model—leader behavior, teacher behavior, and value orientations—which constitute the parameters of this study.

The Organizational Renewal Process

We have defined the organizational renewal (OR) process as the process by which the schools endeavor to attain their goals. For measurement purposes, the |I|D|E|A| Research Division divided the process into three steps: (1) *dialogue* was defined as two-way communication between and among principal and teachers; (2) *decision making* was identified as those school decisions made in a shared situation involving both teachers and the principal; and (3) *action* was defined as some form of change resulting from the first two steps.[10] Organizational renewal, then, was measured in process rather than content terms. During the years 1966–1970, |I|D|E|A| obtained ratings of the degree of progress in developing the dialogue–decision making–action process for eighteen schools joined together as the League of Co-operating Schools. It was against this concept that leader behavior, role conflict and adaptation, and values were tested.

Population

The population for this study was selected from the League of Co-operating Schools, sponsored by the Research Division of the Institute for Development of Educational Activities, Inc. (|I|D|E|A|). The League consisted of eighteen elementary schools and was established in 1965 by John I. Goodlad, Director of the |I|D|E|A| Research Division. Goodlad attempted to select schools which represented diversity in ethnic, socioeconomic, and geographic characteristics representative of similar schools found throughout the nation. Each League school came from a different school district in southern California. The |I|D|E|A| Research Division was attempting to study the process schools use in seeking to attain their goals. As Bentzen has stated:

> The League enterprise serves a dual purpose. One of the aims is to discover the conditions necessary for self-renewing change in the commonplace setting of American schooling. The League is also perceived as a new design for conducting educational research; one that can generate valuable data on planned change, while permitting each of the member schools to fashion and implement their own respective school improvement goals.[11]

Sample

The eighteen members of the League of Cooperating Schools were ranked on composite measures of the organizational renewal (OR) process. Based on these rankings, the four highest schools on the OR measure and the four lowest schools were selected as the sample for the study. It was, therefore, possible to compare the top four and bottom four schools in relation to the measures of leader behavior, role conflict and adaptation, and values.

The following are brief descriptions of each of the procedures used to compile the OR ratings.

League Teacher Reports During the 1968–1969 academic year, designated teachers in each of the eighteen League schools wrote monthly reports describing staff meetings and activities. These reports were subsequently content analyzed for the OR process by the |I|D|E|A| staff.

School Description IV The primary quantitative measure of dialogue, decision making, and action was the School Description IV questionnaire, developed in the school year 1968–1969 by the Research Division of |I|D|E|A|. The development of this measure also required extensive field study and pretesting.

Teacher Interviews These were conducted by |I|D|E|A| staff members in each of the eighteen League schools in the spring of 1969. There was a total of ninety-one respondents, of which eighty-one were complete enough to be tabulated and content analyzed for the OR process.

The Lieberman Questionnaire Another method used in attaining the composite ranking was the Gordon Teacher Leadership Scales, which were empirically tested by Lieberman[12] in the League schools in the spring of 1969. Those items which pertained to dialogue, decision making, and action were selectively extracted and applied to the eighteen schools in terms of the OR criteria. This again led to a ranking of the schools on the basis of OR from the highest to the lowest.

Table 1.1 illustrates the rankings of the eight sample schools as of the fall of 1969 for each of the four procedures discussed above. It should be noted that each of the sample schools appears in the ratings at least twice and in some cases four times.

The entire full-time teaching staffs and each of the eight principals in the sample were encouraged to participate in the study. Since the sample did emanate from the League of Cooperating Schools, no assumptions may be made regarding the degree to which they are representative of school populations in general. The sample consisted of 203 teachers and eight principals. Ninety-five teachers were in the four high OR schools, and 108 were in the four low schools.

Table 1.2 presents the biographical characteristics of the teachers participating in the study. It is readily apparent that women teachers outnumbered men in the sample schools by a ratio of more than five to one. The average age of the participating teachers was thirty-eight, with a mean of ten years teaching experience. The teachers had been at their present schools for about four years and had taught under their present principal for almost three years. In addition, the teachers were members of about three professional educational organizations, most frequently those at the local, state, and national levels.

The teachers' educational background is presented in Table 1.3. A vast majority of the elementary teachers had not yet received the

TABLE 1.1   SUMMARY OF LEAGUE SCHOOL RATINGS

School	League reports	School Description IV	Interviews	Lieberman questionnaire	Composite rating
High OR schools	Woodacres	Seastar Shadyside Woodacres	Seastar Shadyside James Woodacres	Shadyside James Seastar	Seastar Shadyside Woodacres James
Low OR schools	Fairfield Bell Street Mar Villa Independence	Independence Bell Street	Independence	Fairfield Independence Bell Street	Independence Fairfield Bell Street Mar Villa

TABLE 1.2   DESCRIPTION OF PARTICIPATING TEACHING PERSONNEL

School		Sex			Age	Years of teaching experience	Years at present school	Years with present principal	Number of professional organizations
		Male		Female					
		N	%	N	%	$\overline{x}$	$\overline{x}$	$\overline{x}$	$\overline{x}$	$\overline{x}$
High OR schools	Seastar	3	15	19	85	43	14	7	4	4
	Shadyside	1	5	21	95	31	6	2	1	3
	James	4	17	20	83	35	6	3	2	3
	Woodacres	3	12	24	88	31	4	1	1	2
Low OR schools	Fairfield	15	37	22	63	44	13	7	6	3
	Independence	2	8	27	92	40	10	5	2	3
	Bell Street	3	11	18	89	36	11	5	1	2
	Mar Villa	2	10	19	90	39	13	6	4	3
Totals		33	16	170	84	37.5	9.5	4.4	2.6	2.8

master's degree, but about half had taken courses beyond their B.A. None had attained the doctorate.

Since the school principals constituted such a vital dimension in this study, Table 1.4 provides a brief description of their pertinent biographical characteristics. The mean age of the principals was about forty-four, while sixteen years was the average length of time spent in education. They averaged nine years of administrative experience and six years as principal of their present school. All of the principals had

TABLE 1.3   TEACHERS' EDUCATIONAL BACKGROUND

School		BA		BA+		Master's degree		Doctorate	
		N	%	N	%	N	%	N	%
High OR schools	Seastar	4	20	10	50	6	30	0	—
	Shadyside	6	30	14	70	0	—	0	—
	James	7	30	11	48	5	22	0	—
	Woodacres	11	44	12	48	2	8	0	—
Low OR schools	Fairfield	10	28	24	67	2	5	0	—
	Independence	9	35	10	38	7	27	0	—
	Bell Street	9	50	8	44	1	5	0	—
	Mar Villa	9	43	9	43	3	14	0	—
Total		65	34	98	51	26	14	0	—

TABLE 1.4 DESCRIPTION OF PRINCIPALS

OR	Schools	Sex	Age	Administrative experience	Years in education	Years in present school	Educational background
High	Seastar	Male	48	10	19	7	Doctorate
	Shadyside	Male	33	5	9	1	Master's*
	James	Male	41	10	15	3	Master's
	Woodacres	Male	35	3	10	3	Master's*
Low	Fairfield	Male	53	16	25	18	Master's
	Independence	Male	44	6	14	3	Master's
	Bell Street	Male	50	15	23	3	Master's
	Mar Villa	Male	48	8	17	17	Master's
	Principal $\overline{X}$		44	9	16	6	

* Currently working on Doctoral Degree.

the master's degree, one had the doctorate, and two were enrolled in doctoral programs in local universities.

A brief and general description of each of the schools participating in the study, along with a pilot school, is presented in Table 1.5. It may be seen that the age of the school, city population, the number of students and teachers, and mean incomes differed widely from school to school. With two exceptions, the schools were in unified districts and offered grades K–6.

Pilot School

Early in October 1969, the research team selected a League school to serve as a pilot in an attempt to pre-test both the questionnaire package and the procedures of the study. The school was chosen because it had opened early in September and thus had had enough time to settle into its regular operating schedule for the school year. In addition, this school had been ranked in the middle of the League with regard to OR. The research team met with the principal, explained the purpose of the study, and obtained his permission to proceed. An appointment was made for the research team to discuss the study with the faculty later in the month. It was decided that a regular faculty meeting would be used rather than calling a special meeting.

When the research team presented the study at the faculty meeting, there seemed to be genuine interest in the purpose of the study

TABLE 1.5 GENERAL DESCRIPTION OF SAMPLE SCHOOLS BY RANKING IN ORGANIZATIONAL RENEWAL

	High					Low			Pilot
	Seastar	Shadyside	James	Woodacres	Fairfield	Independence	Bell	Mar Villa	Rainbow Hill
Number of teachers	22	32	24	27	37	29	21	21	18
Mean annual teacher salary ($)	11,194	8,959	9,511	8,095	8,630	9,818	10,329	10,793	9,069
Mean teacher family income ($)	19,370	14,723	15,237	16,316	11,746	18,886	17,230	15,190	15,009
Number of students	550	510	682	788	870	860	400	500	570
Population of city	34,000	93,000	711,000	9,500	14,000	175,000	83,000	80,000	40,000
Average family income ($)	12,130	9,734	7,450	13,365	4,553	9,708	11,026	7,250	11,142
Age of school	18	45	28	3	15	66	19	69	8
Grade levels taught	K–6	K–6	3–6	K–6	K–8	K–6	K–6	K–6	K–6
Type of school district	Unif. K–12	Unif. K–12	Unif. K–12	Elem. K–8	Unif. K–12	Unif. K–12	Unif. K–12	Elem. K–6	Unif. K–6

and a lively dialogue followed. The six questionnaires to be used for data collection were then distributed to the teachers. They were given the option of filling them out at faculty meetings or taking them home to complete at their convenience.

The questionnaire phase of the pilot study was completed in October 1969 with 100 percent return. On the basis of the pilot study, there was only a minor revision made in the biographical questionnaire, and, therefore, the approach described above was employed in the sample schools.

The research team returned again to the pilot school in January to pretest the interview phase of the study. Every teacher in the school was interviewed by the research team in an attempt to probe deeper into the quantitative findings. No teacher refused to be interviewed, and all seemed willing to express their ideas to the research team in a candid and frank manner. This approach, too, was followed in the eight sample schools.

Data Collection in the Sample Schools—Phase I

Once the study had been planned and the procedures tried in the pilot school, the research team set up meetings in each of the sample schools so that the purpose of the study might be explained to the principal. It was felt that personal contact was important, both to stress the advantages of the study to each particular school and to establish rapport and understanding with the principals. These meetings usually lasted an hour, and all eight principals seemed interested in participating and pledged their full support to the study. The usual procedure at this time was for the principal to take the research team on a tour of the school, often introducing them to some of the school faculty.

Prior to leaving the school, an appointment was made for the research team to present the study to the school staff at a regularly scheduled faculty meeting, with every attempt being made not to inconvenience the teaching staff with regard to their own time and professional responsibilities. The purpose of the faculty meeting was similar to the meeting with the principal. The research team outlined the study in a short presentation and then answered questions from the staff. The general study was presented as consisting of three parts: the principal, the teachers, and the community. It was further stated that there would be two phases to the study: objective and subjective. The objective phase was to consist of questionnaire responses while the subjective phase would center on interviews, discussions, and observations. The school faculties were also told that the study would constitute the total fall data collection from |I|D|E|A|, which had given its sanction for the study.

The research team also assured the faculty that the findings and recommendations of the study would be presented to them in the early part of the spring. Since knowledge of results was a primary concern of the staff, this point seemed to elicit favorable opinions toward the study.

Four additional approaches were employed by the research team to encourage faculty participation:

The League Reporter For the previous three years, |I|D|E|A| had employed teachers to serve as League Reporters for the purposes of writing reports pertaining to school activities. The research team was able to utilize these individuals as research assistants in that they helped to coordinate the study at the school level. They assisted with the processing and handling of the questionnaires and served as the contacts in the school for the research team.

Research Numbers |I|D|E|A| had instituted another practice which fit into the objective of this study. A research number had been assigned to each teacher for the dual purposes of preserving anonymity and providing continuity of data from one year to another or from one questionnaire to another. Each number consisted of five digits: the first two identified the school, the last three identified the individual. This approach seemed to relieve most of the concerns expressed by the teachers for anonymity, particularly since they were asked to rate their own principal on several measures. The researchers and League Reporters had no access to the key to the numbers and as a consequence had to deal with people through numbers, a difficult task when trying to convince someone to complete all his questionnaires.

Telephone Network The research team also decided to set up a telephone system whereby faculty members could call the researchers when they had questions about the study and, particularly, the questionnaires. Since individuals were going to fill them out at their own convenience, it was felt that both a day and evening number should be provided. The researchers encouraged use of this system at the faculty presentations, as well as by a note attached to each of the questionnaires. This telephone network was used frequently by the teachers in the study, and it proved to be quite helpful in eliciting a high percentage of usable returns.

Questionnaire Schedule The research team made every effort to avoid undue time demands upon the school's personnel with regard to their responses to questionnaires. A questionnaire schedule was set up in collaboration with the League Reporters whereby teachers could complete the questionnaires at their leisure, rather than during regular staff meetings. Since a total of six questionnaires constituted the larger study, the schedule provided for the teachers to complete one per week at a time and place of their own choosing. The first questionnaire requested biographical information and was passed out to the teachers at the faculty meeting where the study was originally introduced. Many turned it in at the end of the meeting while others mailed it in to the researchers or gave it to the League Reporters. The remaining questionnaires were distributed to the teachers by the League Reporters as scheduled by the school questionnaire time table.

After approximately two weeks had elapsed, the research team wrote letters to the faculties to encourage their continued participation and prompt return of the questionnaires. During the month of November, an all-League teachers conference was held in Los Angeles at which time the researchers had an opportunity to converse with many of the teachers participating in the study. After the conference, a two-page letter went out to all the teachers in an attempt to answer many of the questions which had arisen since the onset of the study in the schools.

Beginning in January, the researchers made approximately three trips to each school to encourage completion of the questionnaires, answer any questions which might have developed, and obtain additional data. Thus, every attempt was made to obtain a complete return from each school.

Data Collection in the Sample Schools—Phase II

The second phase of the study involved a subjective approach to the gathering of data requisite to the research design and hypotheses. Recognizing the limitations of questionnaires in providing necessary insights and reasons for behavior, the research team decided upon the unstructured interview procedure in an attempt to probe each of the dimensions of the study through a more comprehensive and in-depth questioning of the respondents.

The research team attempted to interview either all of the teachers in the school or as many as could be scheduled on a given day. The total number interviewed approximated ninety percent of the teachers in the sample and included each principal participating in the study. The interviews were further complemented by informal discussions and observations, though this particular approach was not conducted in any systematic manner due to time limitations. The research team found the interviews to be extremely useful in that they fulfilled their intended purpose of providing illustrative material and insights which were used to complement the findings from the quantitative phase.

Each teacher was interviewed separately when possible, and an attempt was made to meet in a neutral room in the school, rather than the principal's office, which some individuals felt was "bugged." The interview was purposely not tape-recorded to allow the respondents a feeling of freedom in their replies. Notes made by researchers during the interview followed a predetermined format which allowed for individual variations as well as in-depth probing of significant areas identified and uncovered by the respondent. Interviews varied in length, ranging from ten minutes to one hour, depending upon the time available and the significance of the interview. The interviews were subsequently content analyzed.

Limitations of the Study

There are several limitations which govern the generalizability of the findings in this study.

1 All schools in the sample were members of the League of Cooperating Schools, and, therefore, conclusions may be applied only to the eighteen schools in the League. However, it will be recalled that the schools in the League were selected initially to provide a reasonably representative sample of elementary schools generally.

2 All schools in the sample were located in Southern California.

3 The eight schools in the sample were not randomly selected but were chosen on the basis of their high or low ranking in the organizational renewal process.

4 Conclusions were based on teachers' descriptions of only eight principals.

5 The measurement used in this study (the organizational renewal process defined as dialogue, decision making, and action) was developed over a three-year period of concentrated research; however, it still requires further refinement and clarification. Thus, while a considerable effort has been made to insure that no circularity exists,

there may be some overlap since the organizational renewal process involves a wide range of activities and involvements on the part of teachers, administrators, parents, and students. To avoid contamination as far as possible, four separate and independent measures of OR were employed in developing a final composite rating of the eighteen League schools.

6   It has not been established that there is a relationship between organizational renewal and a higher level of student achievement. Therefore, this study is limited to describing the school as a social system and does not attempt to deal with the variable of student achievement. Goodlad set up the League as a means of focusing on the school as the dependent variable in educational improvement.[13] If the setting for learning were improved, he argued, students would be the ultimate beneficiaries.

NOTES

1   Seymour B. Sarason, *The Culture of the School and the Problem of Change*, Allyn and Bacon, Inc., Boston, 1971, p. 2.

2   For outstanding summaries and syntheses of these two approaches see Ralph M. Stogdill, "The Trait Approach to the Study of Leadership," and Stephen P. Hencley, "Situational Behavioral Approach to the Study of Educational Leadership," both of which were presented to the Symposium on Educational Leadership, Phi Delta Kappa, Bloomington, Indiana, 1971. Further information pertaining to these approaches may be found in T. B. Greenfield, "Research on the Behavior of Educational Leaders: Critique of a Tradition," *Alberta Journal of Educational Research,* vol. 14, no. 1, March 1968; Luigi Petrullo and Bernard M. Bass (eds.), *Leadership and Interpersonal Behavior,* Holt, Rinehart and Winston, New York, 1961; Jerrold M. Novotney and Kenneth A. Tye, *The Dynamics of Educational Leadership,* Educational Resource Associates, Inc., Los Angeles, 1973; and Andrew W. Halpin and D. B. Craft, *The Organizational Climate of Schools,* Midwest Administration Center, University of Chicago, Chicago, Illinois, 1963.

3   For a complete discussion of the Getzels–Guba Model, see Jacob W. Getzels, James M. Lipham, and Roald F. Campbell, *Educational Administration as a Social Process,* Harper & Row, New York, 1968.

4   To gain a further understanding of the development and ramifications of the Getzels–Guba Model, see Talcott Parsons, *The Structure of Social Action,* McGraw-Hill, New York, 1937; Talcott Parsons, *The Social System,* Free Press, New York, 1951; Chester I. Barnard, *The*

Functions of the Executive, Harvard University Press, Cambridge, Mass., 1964; Kurt Lewin, *Resolving Social Conflicts,* Harper & Row, New York, 1948; David Riesman et al., *The Lonely Crowd,* Yale University Press, New Haven, 1950; Talcott Parsons and Edward A. Shils (eds.), *Toward a General Theory of Action,* Harvard University Press, Cambridge, Mass., 1951; E. W. Bakke, *Organization and the Individual,* Labor and Management Center, Yale University, New Haven, 1952; Chris Argyris, *Personality and Organization,* Harper & Row, New York, 1957; Chris Argyris, *Integrating the Individual and the Organization,* John Wiley and Sons, New York, 1964; and E. W. Bakke, *The Fusion Process,* Labor and Management Center, Yale University, New Haven, 1953.

5   The most recent summary and description of these studies are contained in Getzels, Lipham, and Campbell, op. cit.

6   James M. Lipham, Critique, Symposium, American Educational Research Association, New York, 1971.

7   Charles C. Wall, "Perceived Leader Behavior of the Elementary School Principal as Related to Educational Goal Attainment," unpublished doctoral dissertation, University of California, Los Angeles, 1970.

8   W. Michael Martin, "Role Conflict and Deviant Adaptation as Related to Educational Goal Attainment," unpublished doctoral dissertation, University of California, Los Angeles, 1970.

9   Arthur Berchin, "Congruency of Values Among Teachers, Principals and Communities as Related to the Goal Attaining Process," unpublished doctoral dissertation, University of California, Los Angeles, 1970.

10 A fourth step, evaluation, was added later in the conceptualization of the |I|D|E|A| Research Division's Study of Educational Change and School Improvement. Details about the conduct of that study and its findings are found in Mary M. Bentzen and associates, *Changing Schools: The Magic Feather Principle,* McGraw-Hill, N.Y., in press.

11 Mary M. Bentzen, "A History of the League of Cooperating Schools," *|I|D|E|A| Reporter,* Fall Quarter, 1969, p. 5.

12 Ann Lieberman, "The Effects of Principal Leadership on Teacher Morale, Professionalism, and Style in the Classroom," unpublished doctoral dissertation, University of California, Los Angeles, 1969.

13 John I. Goodlad, "Staff Development: The League Model," *Theory into Practice,* vol. 11, no. 4, October 1972, pp. 207–214.

CHAPTER 2
THE PRINCIPAL AS A LEADER

The leader behavior of an elementary school principal is one determinant of the ability of a school to attain its stated educational goals. Because the principal is the officially designated head of the school, his actions are the first to be criticized or complimented. It is not uncommon to find that the principal is the first to go when a school encounters problems. It is just as common to discover that changing the principal does not resolve the problem and often intensifies its seriousness. Therefore, a change in school management made without adequate data is not always an appropriate response to a school's problems.

The role a principal is expected to play in a school is usually defined for him by local or state legislative bodies or through tradition. When the principal interprets this role to meet his own needs or those of his staff, there may be serious conflict between what the institution expects from him and how he performs his duties. A greater understanding of the role, personality, institutional expectations, and individual needs may help explain this conflict. The Getzels-Guba Model described in the previous chapter provides a framework within which to examine these relationships carefully.

Each person who occupies a given role specified by an institution personalizes that role. The way in which an elementary school principal personalizes his role can be examined through his behaviors as perceived by his staff. Getzels and Guba describe two broad categories of behaviors that identify the direction in which the principal places the greatest emphasis in fulfilling his role as a leader. The first is identified as *normative style* behaviors. These involve his efforts to fulfill the expectations the school as an organization has for him. An example of a normative leader behavior is found in the principal's relationship with his superiors. If a principal has established good rapport with district personnel who have direct authority over him, and this rapport allows him to attain certain objectives, the principal is demonstrating a normative behavior. He attains his objectives by satisfying his superiors and the demands of the institution rather than looking first at his own needs or those of his staff. Another normative behavior is referred to as Production Emphasis. Here the principal applies pressure on his staff for greater output. He might press his teachers to complete a unit of mathematics on schedule or stress the need for each student to be exposed to the entire social studies program set up by the district before the semester is completed. At this point the reader must be careful not to place value judgments on these behaviors. The question of whether or not it is good to press for greater productivity must be examined in the light of numerous other variables that have an impact on the way the principal behaves.

The second type of behavior discussed by Getzels and Guba is *personal style* leader behaviors. The principal who emphasizes these behaviors is one who is primarily concerned with the needs and expectations of his staff members. Examples include being able to allow teachers the flexibility to explore new instructional methods without the need constantly to monitor their successes or failures. Another example would be the principal's regard for the well being, comfort, and status of his teachers. Here, he respects their ability to make decisions about their own work with children. Again, the reader is cautioned not to judge these behaviors without other evidence regarding the principal's role in the school.

Once it has been established that there are definite types of leader behavior that a principal can exhibit, it is then necessary to discuss how such behavior affects the school as a functioning organization.

This chapter deals with the question, "What is the relationship between a principal's perceived leader behavior and his school's ability to achieve a high level of organizational renewal?" (Notice that we are talking of the principal's behavior *as it is perceived by his staff*. Even if the staff's perceptions are inaccurate, they behave as if the perception represents reality. How the staff sees the principal, then, is a large determinant of how successful he will be in his dealings with them.)

To obtain this information, all teachers in the sample of elementary schools discussed in Chapter 1 were asked to describe their perceptions of their principal's leader behavior. These observations were obtained both by use of a questionnaire and by in-depth interviews held three months later with those teachers who completed the questionnaire. Each principal was also asked to describe his own leader behavior. In addition, teachers and principals were asked to describe the leader behavior of an ideal principal for their school.

The 100-item Leader Behavior Description Questionnaire Form XII (LBDQ-XII) was found to be the most effective instrument available to measure teacher perceptions of principal leader behavior.[1] The LBDQ-XII has twelve separate dimensions, each describing a different leader behavior. Through factor analysis, they divide equally into the normative and personal behaviors described by Getzels. Table 2.1 illustrates the twelve dimensions of leader behavior as described by the LBDQ-XII. Eight of the twelve dimensions are made up of ten separate items on the questionnaire; each of the other four dimensions consists of five individual items. The questionnaire consists of a series of statements about the principal's behavior, and the teacher is asked to rank his principal on a five-point scale ranging from Always to Never. An example of an item from the Consideration dimension is, "He is friendly and approachable." "He keeps the work moving at a rapid pace," and nine other items describe the principal's behavior relative to the Production Emphasis dimension. Other examples of items include: "Things usually turn out as he predicts" (Predictive Accuracy); and "He sees to it that the work of the group is coordinated" (Integration).

To increase the information regarding the principal's perceived real and ideal leader behavior, four variations of the LBDQ-XII were developed. In these variations, the items were not altered but the directions to the respondents were modified so that the desired information was obtained.

First, to determine teachers' perceptions of their principal's leader behavior, the LBDQ-XII was employed without modification. All teachers in the sample of eight elementary schools were asked to complete the questionnaire. This unmodified instrument is referred to as the LBDQ-XII Real in this study. Second, to provide additional information, an alteration was made in the directions of the instrument to allow teachers to indicate what they consider to be the behavior of an "ideal" principal for their school. The responses were compared to the responses given on the LBDQ-XII Real to identify the difference between what teachers perceive to be the principal's leader behavior and what they identify as ideal leader behavior. Because no instruments exist which measure ideal leader behavior in terms which cor-

TABLE 2.1 TWELVE DIMENSIONS OF THE 100-ITEM QUESTIONNAIRE "LEADER BEHAVIOR DESCRIPTION QUESTIONNAIRE FORM XII"

Leader behavior orientation	Number	Dimension	Description
	1	Representation	Speaks and acts as the representative of the group
	2	Persuasiveness	Uses persuasion and argument effectively; exhibits strong convictions
Normative (Factor I)	3	Initiation of Structure	Clearly defines own role, and lets followers know what is expected
	4	Role Assumption	Actively exercises the leadership role rather than surrendering leadership to others
	5	Production Emphasis	Applies pressure for productive output
	6	Superior Orientation	Maintains cordial relations with superiors; has influence with them; is striving for higher status
	7	Demand Reconciliation	Reconciles conflicting demands and reduces disorder to system
	8	Tolerance of Uncertainty	Is able to tolerate uncertainty and postponement without anxiety or upset
Personal (Factor II)	9	Tolerance of Freedom	Allows followers scope for initiative, decision, and action
	10	Consideration	Regard for comfort, well-being, status, and contribution of followers
	11	Predictive Accuracy	Exhibits foresight and ability to predict outcomes accurately
	12	Integration	Maintains a closely knit organization; resolves intermember conflict

respond to the twelve dimensions of the LBDQ-XII, the use of this instrument with the alterations in directions (called the LBDQ-XII Ideal) was essential to keep all data compatible with the theoretical framework of this study.[2] It must be noted that only the basic directions were changed; no items were altered in any manner.

Each principal in the sample of schools was also asked to participate. On a third variation of the instrument, he was asked to rate his own behavior on the same twelve dimensions as those on which his teachers rated him. Again, the only modification of the LBDQ-XII concerned changes in the basic directions. The directions were modified in a fourth version so that each principal would have the opportunity to describe what he felt to be the ideal behavior of a principal in his school. Again, only directions were changed, and the same twelve dimensions used in the LBDQ-XII Real were studied.

The Relationship of the Principal's Behavior to OR

Several critical questions formed the basis for the hypotheses to be tested in this study. The first question was, "Is there any relationship between the principal's style of leader behavior and the school's organizational renewal ranking?" We hypothesized that high OR schools would have principals who tended to use personal style behaviors more than normative and that principals in low OR schools would be more likely to be normative style leaders.

Teachers' responses to the LBDQ Real provided the data to answer this question. The individual teacher scores for each school were averaged, and the mean school scores for the high OR group were compared to the mean school scores for the low OR group.

As a result of this analysis, it is possible to say that a principal's leader behavior style does have some relationship to his school's OR ranking. Our hunch proved to be correct, as the principals of all four high OR schools were ranked higher by their teachers on personal style leader behaviors than on normative style behaviors. In three of the four low OR schools, teachers rated their principal higher on normative style leader behavior than on personal style behavior. The principal of one low OR school was rated higher on personal style than on normative style leader behavior. Figure 2.1 shows how each of the principals in the sample was rated by his teachers.

Teachers in three of the four low OR schools were in relative agreement in their perceptions of their principal's leader behavior. The

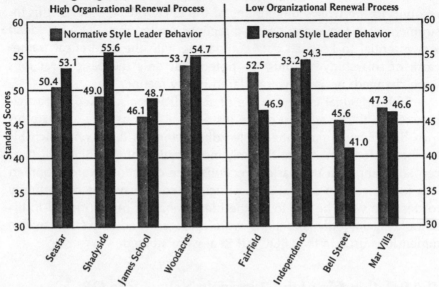

FIGURE 2.1   TEACHER PERCEPTION OF PRINCIPAL LEADER
BEHAVIOR AS MEASURED BY THE LBDQ-XII

production emphasis dimension, a normative style leader behavior
concerned with the amount of pressure employed by the leader to
gain a higher level of output, was rated as the most frequently employed leader behavior by the faculties of Fairfield, Bell Street, and
Mar Villa. These teachers gave their principals the lowest ratings on
personal style dimensions. The teachers in the fourth low OR school,
Independence, perceived their principal's leader behavior as being
personal in style and rated him highest on the Consideration dimension. His lowest rating was on the normative style dimension of Representation, which deals with the principal's ability to speak and act as
a representative of the group.

It should be noted that in all four high organizational renewal
schools, the principal's *least* used behavior was a normative style dimension. However, while it was found that principals in high OR
schools did employ personal style leader behavior, there were numerous variations on how principals were rated on the various dimensions within the personal style category. For example, teachers in
Shadyside (see Appendix A for a description of each of the schools in
the study) rated their principal highest on the Consideration dimension, while teachers in James School rated their principal highest on

the Tolerance of Freedom dimension. Both are personal style leader behaviors. Such variations may reflect the different emphasis placed on a given dimension of leader behavior by each principal. One principal may feel it is far more important for him to allow his faculty to explore and initiate decisions and actions (the Tolerance of Freedom dimension) while another may view reconciliation of conflicting demands (Demand Reconciliation) as needing his attention. It is also possible that emphasis on one dimension may indicate a weakness in another dimension, since the principal may concentrate his efforts in those areas where he feels most comfortable and avoid those behaviors that are most difficult for him to deal with effectively.

It is also possible that an individual teacher's perception of a principal's leader behavior is influenced by such factors as teacher age, grade level taught, and teaching experience. Such biographical information had been obtained from the teachers and through the use of correlation analysis it was determined that there was no significant relationship between these variables and the teacher's perception of principal's leader behavior. Thus, the data from this study indicate that, for example, older teachers do not perceive principals differently than younger teachers. Also, teachers who have had more experience in the classroom than other teachers do not have a different perception of their principal's leader behavior.

Interviews with the teachers in the eight schools tended to confirm the ratings of principals indicated by the scores of the LBDQ-XII Real. During the interviews, teachers were asked to describe their principal's leader behavior. Notes were taken of the teachers' remarks, and these were analyzed for content against the twelve dimensions of the LBDQ-XII. This was accomplished by extracting all comments regarding the principal's leader behavior made by teachers in the interviews and listing them. Each comment was matched to one of the twelve dimensions of the LBDQ-XII, and then all replies were grouped by school and reviewed to determine the general faculty attitude toward the principal. By comparing these comments to the data supplied by the instrument, it was determined that the comments made by teachers in the interviews generally supported the data provided on the LBDQ-XII Real.

The Ideal Principal

After confirming that there is indeed a relationship between the principal's leader behavior style and the schools' OR ranking, our next question was, "Is there a set of ideal principal leader behaviors on which all teachers would agree?" We hypothesized that regardless of their school's OR ranking, there would be certain leader behaviors that all teachers would endorse as ideal for their school.

The answer to this question was based on data collection from the LBDQ-XII Ideal. Mean scores for high OR schools were compared with those from low OR schools (a 2-tail t-test; see Glossary, under "t-test," for further discussion). Based on this analysis, it was found that teachers and principals in both high and low OR schools showed no significant disagreement on their perceptions of ideal principal leader behavior on nine of the twelve LBDQ-XII dimensions. Even though there was no disagreement, no clear pattern of desired ideal leader behavior emerged when the ratings of teachers from both high and low OR schools were compiled.

On the remaining three dimensions there were significant differences between teachers in high OR schools and teachers in low organizational renewal schools. Teachers in high OR schools perceived an ideal principal as being significantly higher on the dimensions of Tolerance of Uncertainty and Tolerance of Freedom than did teachers in low OR schools. These two dimensions are personal style behaviors and reflect the teacher's desire to have the opportunity to explore new ideas in the classroom without administrative involvement. It may be that teachers in high OR schools have found they function much more effectively when not under constant administrative supervision and so want a principal to demonstrate these behaviors. Teachers in the low-ranking OR schools felt that an ideal principal should stress the dimension of Production Emphasis at a significantly higher level than did teachers in the high-ranking schools. The desire on the part of teachers in low OR schools for a principal who emphasizes this dimension is very interesting. It is an indication that they feel they need constant support and reinforcement from their administrator. It is somewhat of an admission that they lack self-direction and motivation to function independently in the classroom.

The Match between Real and Ideal

The third question we wanted answered was, "Does the congruency or lack of congruency between the ideal principal behavior that the teachers want and the perceived behavior of their real principal have any relationship to the school's OR ranking?" We hypothesized that in high OR schools the principal's real leader behavior would be closer to the ideal his teachers wanted than it would be in low OR schools.

To test this question, real and ideal scores for each school were analyzed using a t-test for correlated means (see Glossary). Table 2.2 lists the twelve LBDQ dimensions and those schools in which real–ideal differences were found. Schools are not included in this table if there were no significant differences between real and ideal principal leader behavior as perceived by the teachers. The four high organizational renewal schools showed significant differences between real and ideal leader behavior on seventeen comparisons. In contrast, the four

TABLE 2.2   AGREEMENT AMONG SAMPLE SCHOOLS REGARDING DIFFERENCES BETWEEN LBDQ-XII REAL AND IDEAL QUESTIONNAIRES ON EACH OF TWELVE DIMENSIONS (MATCHED PAIRS— 2-TAIL T-TESTS)

Dimension	High Organizational Renewal Schools	Low Organizational Renewal Schools
Representation		
Persuasion	Shadyside‡ James School‡	Fairfield* Independence* Bell Street* Mar Villa†
Initiation of Structure	Shadyside‡ James School‡ Woodacres*	Independence* Bell Street* Mar Villa†
Role Assumption	Shadyside† James School‡	Fairfield‡ Bell Street* Mar Villa*
Production Emphasis	James School‡	
Superior Orientation	James School†	Mar Villa*
Demand Reconciliation	Shadyside‡ James School‡	Fairfield† Independence* Bell Street† Mar Villa*
Tolerance of Uncertainty	Woodacres*	Fairfield* Bell Street* Mar Villa*
Tolerance of Freedom		Fairfield* Bell Street* Mar Villa*
Consideration	James School†	Fairfield† Mar Villa†
Predictive Accuracy	James School*	Fairfield* Mar Villa*
Integration	Shadyside† James School†	Fairfield* Independence* Bell Street† Mar Villa‡

* Significant at .05 level.
† Significant at .01 level.
‡ Significant at .001 level.

low OR schools revealed twenty-nine separate significant differences between real and ideal leader behavior. It can therefore be stated that in the high organizational renewal schools, as perceived by the teachers from these schools, a greater degree of congruency between real and ideal principal leader behavior was found.

Of the four high OR schools, one school, Seastar, had no significant differences between real and ideal leader behavior on any of the twelve dimensions. The other three high OR schools showed significant differences between the real and ideal leader behavior on the Initiation of Structure dimension (i.e., the leader clearly defines his own role and lets others know what is expected of them). This suggests that the teachers in these schools believe that ideally their principal should be more definitive in what his function is as the designated leader of the school and, as a result, make clear what is expected of them. Three of the four low OR faculties scored similarly on this dimension. There were no other dimensions among the four high OR schools where there was agreement among more than two schools on any one dimension.

All four low OR schools rated their principals lower than they ideally wanted on three dimensions: Persuasiveness, Demand Reconciliation, and Integration. This suggests that the teachers in all four of these schools believe that their principals could employ a greater commitment to concepts and ideas he believes in and a greater facility in persuading his teachers that his ideas are worthwhile and could give greater attention to reconciling conflicting demands among teachers and reducing these demands to systematic order. They also indicated the importance they place on a close-knit organization in which there is less tension among employees.

INDIVIDUAL SCHOOL PROFILES

To provide a more detailed picture of the influence of the principal's leader behavior on the organizational renewal ranking of the school, each of the sample schools is discussed separately in the following section. The information is drawn from both questionnaires and interviews, and typical teacher comments are included. The high OR schools are presented first and then the low OR schools. Definitions of leader behavior discussed here have been provided in Table 2.1.

High Organizational Renewal Schools

Seastar Elementary School The principal of Seastar was perceived as a personal style leader and was rated highest on the Tolerance of Freedom dimension. His second highest rating was the normative dimension of Persuasiveness. The principal was apparently fulfilling the needs and expectations of the teachers, for, of all eight sample schools, Seastar revealed the greatest congruency between teachers' perception of real and ideal principal leader behavior (see Figure 2.2). There were no significant differences between real and ideal principal leader behavior on any of the twelve dimensions. In addition, Seastar showed less difference than any other school between real and ideal leader behavior on seven dimensions: Demand Reconciliation, Persuasion, Tolerance of Freedom, Role Assumption, Production Emphasis, Predictive Accuracy, and Superior Orientation.

   The teachers in Seastar perceived their principal as exerting virtually no pressure on them for production, and this de-emphasis was

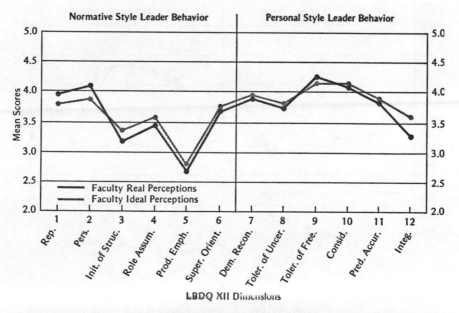

FIGURE 2.2   SEASTAR ELEMENTARY SCHOOL FACULTY PERCEPTION OF PRINCIPAL BEHAVIOR AS MEASURED BY THE LBDQ-XII

ideally what the teachers wanted from the principal. A typical remark from teachers during individual interviews was: "He does not stress output in terms of what I am doing in the classroom." One teacher commented, "Isn't it interesting that our principal does not emphasize production, yet in our country we press hard for greater output as a measure of success. In this school there is practically no pressure for production, yet we are very successful."

Visits to individual classrooms in this school and informal discussions with teachers indicated a considerable amount of innovation and creative effort on the part of both teachers and principal. The staff appeared highly motivated and self-directed.

Shadyside Elementary School The Shadyside principal was also considered a personal style leader with his highest ratings on the personal dimensions of Tolerance of Freedom, Consideration, and Tolerance of Uncertainty. The faculty of Shadyside indicated that there were significant differences between real and ideal principal leader behavior on five of the twelve dimensions (see Figure 2.3). The interviews sug-

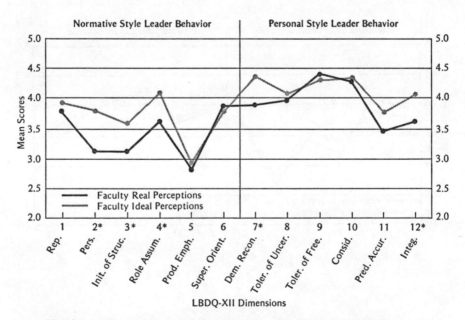

*Significant difference between real-ideal perception of principal leader behavior

FIGURE 2.3 SHADYSIDE ELEMENTARY SCHOOL FACULTY PERCEPTION OF PRINCIPAL LEADER BEHAVIOR AS MEASURED BY THE LBDQ-XII

gested that the dimension of Persuasion represented the area of greatest dissatisfaction. Typical teacher comments were:

"Not very persuasive."
"Comes across very weak."
"Generally we need a much stronger principal."
"May not need to be persuasive with this faculty, we are self-directed."
"Sometimes at faculty meetings . . . will present something and it dies without comment."

Of all eight sample schools, Shadyside exhibited the greatest congruency between real and ideal leader behavior on the normative dimension of Representation. The teachers were obviously satisfied with the principal's ability to speak for them and represent their interests.

Although Shadyside was ranked high in organizational renewal, informal discussions with teachers and visits to their classrooms revealed that they did not believe that they were very innovative. Even so, they had established a learning center which allowed children free access to a wide variety of materials not normally found in a classroom. Their learning center was the most innovative and advanced of any established by schools in the sample. The faculty was young and eager to try new ideas but appeared to need an outside stimulus which the principal did not seem to be able to offer. The principal's low rating on Production Emphasis may be another indication of this need.

James Elementary School   The greatest number of significant differences between real and ideal leader behavior of any of the high OR schools appeared in James School (see Figure 2.4). The principal was considered personal in style with his highest rating on the Tolerance of Freedom dimension. However, teachers expressed dissatisfaction with the principal's leader behavior on nine dimensions, with the dissatisfaction spread over both normative style and personal style leader behaviors. Some typical comments from teachers during the interview were:

"I need and would like to have much more direction in what I am doing in my classroom."
"He allows considerable freedom to the point of laissez faire."
"Very lax in authority."
"He is not very persuasive with the faculty. However, he knows that he is the authority and there is little dispute with what he wants."

Even though there was a great deal of negative feeling about the principal, positive attitudes were also expressed.

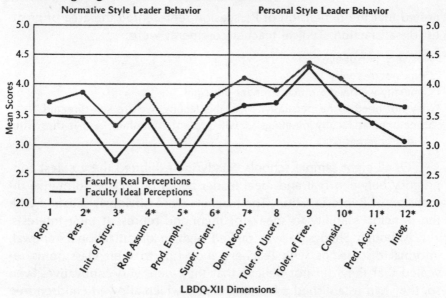

*Significant difference between real-ideal perception of principal leader behavior

FIGURE 2.4   JAMES ELEMENTARY SCHOOL FACULTY PERCEPTION OF PRINCIPAL LEADER BEHAVIOR AS MEASURED BY THE LBDQ-XII

"He is approachable and helpful to me when I ask for help."
"He feels confident about what he is doing, he really believes in what is going on here."

It should be noted that at the time the questionnaires were being completed in this school, a teacher's strike was pending and communication between the principal (representing the administration position) and the teachers (representing the union position) was strained. Such a situation could easily have influenced the teachers when completing the questionnaires and could have caused them to exaggerate their expectations of an ideal principal. However, the disagreements between the union and the school district were settled without a strike, and the teachers and principal were able to reestablish a working relationship rather quickly. By the time the interviews were held two months later, the strike tension had subsided and the issue was almost forgotten. One could speculate that such might not have been the case had the teachers and principal been unable to work together prior to the strike threat.

Woodacres Elementary School   The Woodacres principal was perceived as a personal style leader. He was rated highest on Tolerance of Freedom, Demand Reconciliation, Consideration, and the normative dimension of Representation. The faculty of Woodacres indicated congruency between principal real and ideal leader behavior for ten of the twelve dimensions on the LBDQ-XII (Figure 2.5). Significant differences were found in the dimensions of Initiation of Structure and Tolerance of Uncertainty. While there was some dissatisfaction among a small group of faculty members, the principal appeared to be meeting the teachers' basic expectations concerning his role. Typical comments from teachers regarding the principal were as follows:

"The principal is just great. He allows considerable flexibility in our classes. He listens to all viewpoints and is quite helpful."

Even so, negative comments were also made.

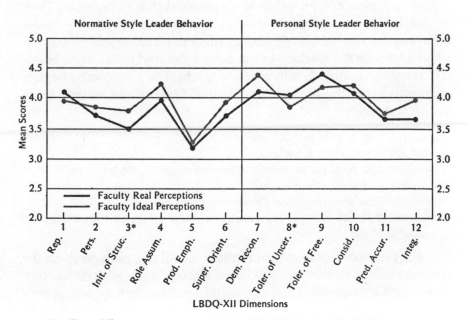

*Significant difference between real-ideal perception of principal leader behavior

FIGURE 2.5   WOODACRES ELEMENTARY SCHOOL FACULTY PERCEPTION OF PRINCIPAL LEADER BEHAVIOR AS MEASURED BY THE LBDQ-XII

"In a school like this one where community pressure is so strong, we need a strong leader who can support us. He does not stand up for us."

Woodacres was attempting many new teaching techniques that were considered radical by some segments of the community. Each time an article about the school appeared in the local press, pressure from the community created an atmosphere of tension. It was difficult to develop an accurate portrait of this school as the teachers, principal, and community were frequently at odds. It was indicated by several teachers in interviews that the community pressure may actually have unfavorably influenced their perception of the principal's leader behavior.

Low Organizational Renewal Schools

Fairfield Elementary School   Fairfield's faculty rated the principal's real leader behavior as normative and considered it to be significantly below what they would have liked from an ideal principal on eight dimensions (Figure 2.6), including all six personal style dimensions. Thus, the teachers felt the principal was not employing personal style leader behaviors the way they perceived an ideal principal would. The interviews held with the teachers in this school exposed widespread hostility toward the principal, with very few teachers making complimentary comments about the principal as a leader. Some of the remarks made by teachers were:

"He provides no help in instructional leadership."
"Not in the classroom much at all."
"Uses force and pressure to convince teacher what should be done."
"Very weak in dealing with people."
"At least ten teachers have been thrown out of his office."[3]
"Tolerance of freedom is not his strategy, but just a lack of concern for the teacher in the classroom."

The principal and faculty of Fairfield school had not agreed on the specific goals they wished to achieve through their educational program. Visits to classrooms and discussions with teachers regarding their classroom goals and their goals in the school in general revealed virtually no creativity or innovation throughout the school. In fact, of a faculty of thirty-seven, only two teachers were attempting innovative programs, one who was soon retired and the other an intern from a nearby teachers' college.

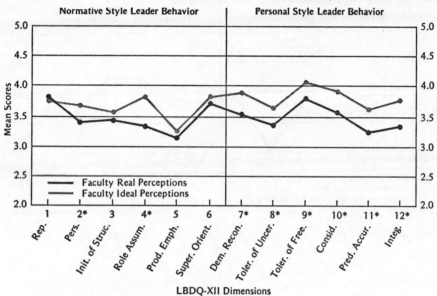

The Principal as a Leader 35

*Significant difference between real-ideal perception of principal leader behavior

FIGURE 2.6 FAIRFIELD ELEMENTARY SHOOL FACULTY PERCEPTION OF PRINCIPAL BEHAVIOR AS MEASURED BY THE LBDQ-XII

Independence Elementary School Independence was unique among the low OR schools. The principal was perceived as personal in style and rated highest on Consideration and Tolerance of Freedom. There were only four dimensions with significant differences between teachers' perceptions of the principal's real leader behavior and that of an ideal leader. As shown in Figure 2.7, two of these four dimensions were from the normative style leader behavior dimensions (Persuasiveness and Initiation of Structure) and two from the personal style leader behavior dimensions (Demand Reconciliation and Integration).

Teacher interviews revealed mixed feelings about the principal as a leader. One faction of the faculty felt he was a superb leader, while another group felt that it was the strength of the teachers themselves which accounted for the school's success. Typical comments from teachers included:

"When he is here, he comes into all the classrooms. But he is too involved in outside activities."

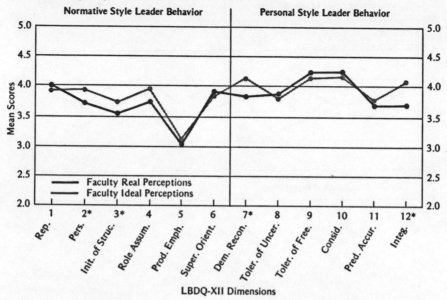

*Significant difference between real-ideal perception of principal leader behavior

FIGURE 2.7   INDEPENDENCE ELEMENTARY SCHOOL FACULTY PERCEPTION OF PRINCIPAL LEADER BEHAVIOR AS MEASURED BY THE LBDQ-XII

"This seems to be a well-functioning organization."

"He doesn't give me very much help in the classroom."

"He never puts pressure on us to do anything specific. We have considerable freedom."

"He is a very strong, warm-hearted leader and makes us feel that our opinions are worthwhile. He is very considerate of all of us personally."

Visits to classrooms in Independence revealed a variety of activities, both innovative and conventional. There was a large group of teachers who were neither conventional nor particularly innovative. It should be noted that prior to this study the faculty of Independence had been divided into two buildings, several blocks apart, and that the organizational renewal score for this school had been derived during the last year of the divided situation.

Bell Street Elementary School   The Bell Street principal was considered a normative style leader though his highest rating was the personal dimension, Tolerance of Freedom. The faculty of Bell Street (Figure 2.8)

identified seven real leader behavior dimensions that were significantly different from what they ideally wanted. Four of these were personal style behaviors and three were normative style leader behaviors. Teachers interviewed in this school generally voiced displeasure regarding the principal's leader behavior. Some were extremely hostile ("He is the Peter Principle personified"), while others expressed their opinion less forcefully ("He just doesn't understand what we are doing").

However, without exception, every teacher in the school stated in the interviews that despite the principal's obvious weaknesses as a leader he was a warm and considerate human being. This probably is indicated by the congruency between their real and ideal perceptions on the dimensions of Consideration and Representation. All teachers said that he loved children and seemed to direct his energy toward their welfare. Visits to classrooms revealed they were mostly conventional with few innovations. Three classrooms, though, were very innovative and seemed to meet with the principal's approval.

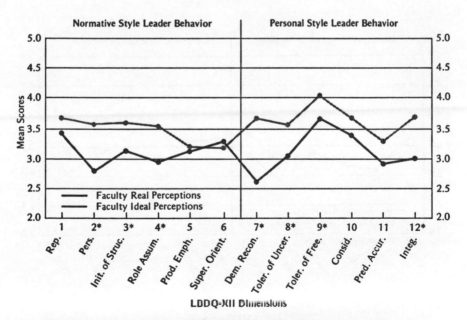

*Significant difference between real-ideal perception of principal leader behavior

FIGURE 2.8 BELL STREET ELEMENTARY SCHOOL FACULTY PERCEPTION OF PRINCIPAL LEADER BEHAVIOR AS MEASURED BY THE LBDQ-XII

Mar Villa Elementary School   Mar Villa was the lowest of the eight schools in the sample in terms of congruency between faculty perceptions of real and ideal leader behavior. In Figure 2.9, the ten dimensions that were in dispute are graphically depicted. When the absolute magnitude of the differences between the means on the LBDQ-XII Real and Ideal were ranked from one to eight (representing the sample population), Mar Villa ranked seventh or eighth on every dimension. There were only two dimensions where the teachers expressed satisfaction with the principal's leader behavior. The teachers were satisfied with the de-emphasis on productive output (Production Emphasis) that the principal exhibited and also with his public relations ability, as evidenced by their positive rating of him on the Representation dimension.

Interviews held with each teacher in Mar Villa confirmed widespread dissatisfaction with the principal as a leader. Typical comments from teachers about the principal were:

"I have been here many years. I can't think of anything positive to say."

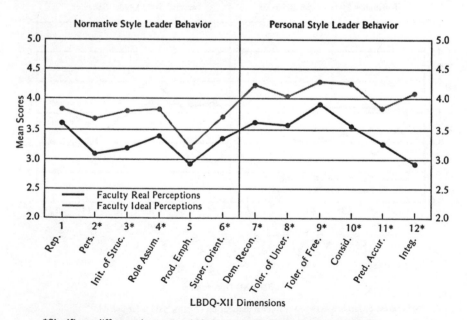

*Significant difference between real-ideal perception of principal leader behavior

FIGURE 2.9   MAR VILLA ELEMENTARY SCHOOL FACULTY PERCEPTION OF PRINCIPAL LEADER BEHAVIOR AS MEASURED BY THE LBDQ-XII

"I don't think he would back us up if a problem developed such as with the
 community."
"The faculty morale is low. There are no social activities among teachers at
 this school."
"He rarely visits my classroom, so yes, I am free to do whatever I want."
"There are four of us who are leaving because of dissatisfaction with the principal. At a faculty meeting he wrote our names on the blackboard so
 everyone would know who we were. Everyone already knew."
"He cannot communicate his ideas."

Visits to classrooms in this school revealed almost no innovations.
A massive building remodeling program had just started at Mar Villa
which was forcing new teaching methods upon the teachers by altering
the physical arrangement of the classrooms. This was very upsetting to
most of the faculty and could have been the cause of some of the dissatisfaction with the principal. It was the principal who was heavily
promoting these changes.

CONCLUSIONS AND RECOMMENDATIONS

The three questions examined in this study were created to provide an
answer to the general question, "What is the relationship between a
principal's perceived leader behavior and his school's organizational
renewal ranking?" From the data discussed here, it can be concluded
that a high organizational renewal school will have a principal who
emphasizes the personal dimensions in his leader behavior and has
greater concern for his teaching staff than he does for institutional
maintenance. A characteristic of a low OR school is that it will have
a principal who de-emphasizes staff needs in favor of institutional
needs and expectations.

Two other conclusions based on the results of this study can be
summarized briefly. First, critical insights are not revealed by asking
teachers in either high or low OR schools to describe an ideal principal's leader behavior. With the exception of only three dimensions,
teachers in the sample of schools studied, whether they were high or
low organizational renewal schools, had a similar view of ideal principal leader behavior.

Second, age, sex, length of teaching experience, length of time at
present school, and educational background have no bearing upon
how a teacher will perceive the principal's real or ideal leader behavior. Younger teachers do not differ from older teachers in their
perceptions of a principal's leader behavior. The same perceptions of

principal leader behavior are found among teachers with only a few years of experience or many years of experience.

It is also possible to say that if there is congruence between teachers' perceptions of their principal's real and ideal leader behavior, the school will more likely than not demonstrate a high level of organizational renewal. There is less likelihood that a school will demonstrate a high OR level if there is a lack of congruency between teachers' perceptions of their principal's real and ideal leader behavior.

As a result of the data presented here, it is possible to pose several recommendations. These recommendations are made in an attempt to expand on our findings and to point to areas in which schools can use the principal's leader behavior as a useful data source for determining effective organizational renewal.

Our data indicate that an attempt should be made by schools concerned with implementing innovative practices to insure that the principal is oriented behaviorally toward staff needs and expectations rather than institutional needs and expectations.

A high level of organizational renewal cannot be mandated through district directions, but the principal, as the officially designated leader, has considerable power to either encourage or discourage the OR process. The principal must recognize staff needs for such things as the opportunity to try new methods without the fear of being reprimanded. When a principal is consciously aware of his teachers' professional qualifications to instruct children, there is a much greater opportunity for the school as a unit to attain its desired objectives. If, on the other hand, the principal is more concerned with making a good impression on the district superintendent, maintaining his role as the authority figure, and pushing his faculty for productive output, there is less opportunity for faculty involvement and, therefore, the OR process will suffer.

Principals need to be fully aware of their teachers' perception of their leader behaviors. Once these behaviors are known, free and open discussion should take place between principal and teachers regarding those behaviors that are creating dissatisfaction. Even if an alteration in the behavior in question is not possible, its exposure and discussion will often prevent undesirable conflicts from arising.

It is frequently recommended that a principal should attempt to achieve a perfect balance between institutional requirements and staff needs. This study does not support that recommendation. A balance of the two behavior orientations will create a bland status quo compromise. To achieve goals, to implement change, and to create a dynamic enthusiastic environment in which to work, a principal must be more heavily concerned with his staff's needs than he is with the institutional requirements. Getzels goes one step further in that he suggests dynamic leaders should have the ability to alter their leader behavior to suit the situation. Getzels identifies the leader who can alter his own behavior to meet the situation as being a "transactional" leader. This means that the principal takes some of the normative behaviors and combines them with personal style behaviors in an effort to continue his leadership role. It can be speculated that such ability on the part of a principal will insure his school's movement toward desired objectives. When the principal and his staff become complacent with a given leader style then stagnation begins to appear. A principal should have the flexibility to stress one type of leader orientation but still use another behavior orientation when he deems it necessary. The principal of Seastar Elementary School is an example of this flexibility. While he gives his staff the freedom to explore new teaching methods, he also exerts normative behaviors when he feels they have gone far enough and need to reflect on their progress or lack of progress. When, in his judgment, the staff has reflected on their current position or have achieved desired interim objectives, he again provides an atmosphere of freedom to move ahead. Such changes based upon situational needs may be thought of as manipulative. This would be true if, through changing his leader behavior, he directed his faculty in specific activities that they found disruptive or unproductive in their efforts to attain certain goals. It would also be considered manipulative if he provided the opportunity for progress but then specified the type of progress and the direction teachers are to follow in attaining predetermined goals.

Once it has been determined what teachers perceive their principal's "real" leader behavior to be, the next task is to compare these perceptions against what they would like to have in an "ideal" principal for their school. It may be found, for example, that a principal is perceived as having a normative style orientation when teachers want a personal style principal. Such a situation might well be the cause of a great deal of difficulty in the school. However, revealing this information to both staff and principal is dysfunctional unless follow-up activities are planned and implemented.

The results of the "real" and "ideal" scores on the LBDQ-XII must be analyzed carefully to determine which of the twelve dimensions show the greatest difference in scores. It probably will be found that several of the dimensions have perfect congruence between what teachers perceive to be "real" and "ideal" leader behavior. Teachers may feel strongly about only three or four dimensions. When it is known exactly which dimensions are in dispute, the others can be ignored and all attention given to those where basic disagreement exists. Open and continuous dialogue is now necessary between teachers and principal. Through such dialogue, some decisions should be forthcoming which will begin to close the gap between "real" and "ideal" principal leader behavior. The next step is to implement some action to resolve the disagreements. The final step is to evaluate the process to see if, in fact, changes have taken place in either faculty needs and expectations or the principal's interpretation of his own role as leader. Thus, the dialogue–decision making–action sequence which we have defined as organizational renewal (see Chapter 1) is put into operation to resolve problems which might well be limiting the school's capability to achieve desired objectives.

While it is recommended that "real" and "ideal" principal leader behavior be examined together, it is not recommended that "ideal" behavior be analyzed independently. As the data have shown, this measure seems to have its greatest utility when compared with "real" behavior and seems to reveal little when taken separately.

NOTES

1　For details regarding this instrument see: Ralph M. Stogdill, "Manual for the Leader Behavior Description Questionnaire Form XII," The Ohio State University, Bureau of Business Education, Columbus, Ohio, 1963.

2　This is not intended to imply that instruments are not available to test for ideal leader behavior. The original LBDQ developed in 1957 by Halpin and Coons does have such a companion instrument, but it does not discriminate between the desired dimensions being tested in this study.

3　Several teachers admitted to this fact and willingly described the circumstances surrounding the issue.

CHAPTER 3
ROLE-PERSONALITY CONFLICT AND MODES OF ADAPTATION

One of the more perplexing tasks of leadership is mediating the expectations of an organization and the desires and preferences of its employees in a way that is both productive for the organization and satisfying for the employee. As Argyris states,

> ... if the organization's goals are to be achieved, and knowing that both will always strive for self-actualization, it follows that effective leadership is "fusing" the individual and the organization in such a way that both simultaneously obtain self-actualization. The process of the individual using the organization to fulfill his needs and simultaneously the organization "using" the individuals to achieve its demands has been called by Bakke the fusion process.[1]

In the educational setting, we find such a situation existing between the expectations of the school or system and the needs of the teachers and principals. The following portion of the Getzels model is illustrative:

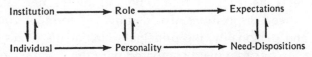

The institution defines certain roles to be enacted within the organization, which in turn create expectations that the actors who play these roles will have to fulfill. However, since each individual actor brings to his role his own personality, he has certain needs which he expects to be fulfilled in the performance of his role. In reality, we are unlikely to find absolute compatibility between institutional expectations and individual needs, and therefore a certain degree of strain or conflict is likely to exist between the two, which we call *role–personality conflict*.

Such conflict requires some form of adaptation or adjustment on the part of either the individual or the organization.

Getzels, Lipham, and Campbell[2] state that an individual encountering this role–personality conflict can adapt one of three forms of behavior: (1) he may choose "role adaptation," whereby be allies himself with the expectations of the organization or school and does not seek fulfillment of his personal needs through his work; (2) he may choose what Maslow calls "self-actualization," in which he rejects organizational expectations and expresses his own need-dispositions; or (3) he may choose some form of compromise between the two. Since the first two behavioral modes rarely appear in a pure form, it is the third which is most frequently found in reality, and we thus observe a greater or lesser degree of adaptation of "self-actualization" to organizational demands.

We have identified three kinds of role–personality conflict:

Expectational role–personality conflict is the discrepancy between what the principal expects the teacher role in the school to be and what the teacher perceives the principal's expectation for that role to be. To measure this conflict, we asked principals to identify their specific expectations for teachers. For example, principals responded to the questionnaire item, "I expect my teachers to adapt curricular guides to the needs and interests of pupils." At the same time, teachers were asked what they perceived to be their principal's expectations for his teachers. In this case, the questionnaire item was reworded to read, "My principal expects me to adapt curricular guides to the needs and interests of pupils." Any incongruity between the principal's and the teachers' responses was defined as expectational conflict.

Actual role–personality conflict is the conflict between what the principal expects the teachers' role to be and the teachers' statements of their own need-dispositions. To identify this form of conflict between role and personality, the principal's statements of his expectations for the teacher role were compared with the teachers' own indications of what they needed and desired. Statements of the teachers' needs were obtained by the same questionnaire items used to measure expectational conflict, but the items were again reworded. For example, the item cited above now read, "I would like to adapt curricular guides to the needs and interests of pupils." Identifying role–personality conflict in this form draws upon the work of Seeman[3] in his important study of Ohio superintendents. This perspective holds that certain expectations are attached to the teacher role, and in any given school the principal is the actor who defines at least one set of significant and legitimate expectations for that role. Since this type of role–personality conflict is a direct confrontation between institutional expectations and individual needs, it fits most closely into the Getzels model.

Perceptual role–personality conflict is the difference between what the teachers perceive to be the principal's expectations for their role and their own statement of needs. This perspective emanates from the work of Stouffer[4] who described his subjects as perceiving a range of "permissiveness" in resolving role conflict situations. This conflict was identified by comparing the teachers' perceptions of the principal's expectations (obtained through their responses to items prefaced, "My principal expects me to . . .") with their statements of their own needs (items prefaced, "I would like to . . .). This type of role–personality conflict is potentially the most straining for a social system since it exists in the "eye of the beholder" and is therefore a powerful motivator for individual and group behavior.

The Teacher Behavior Questionnaire (TBQ)[5] was used to obtain measures of these three kinds of role–personality conflict. As can be seen from the illustrations given above, the items remained constant for all three measures and only the direction of the item was changed. The principal responded to items which began, "I expect the teacher to . . ." and the teacher responded to items which began "My principal expects the teacher to . . ." and "I would like to . . .," but the basic items for both read, ". . . feel free to be selective about participation in community affairs, choosing those activities, if any, which are interesting and enjoyable," or ". . . leave the conduct of administrative affairs to the discretion of the principal."

As stated above, whenever there is conflict between the expectations of the institution and the need-dispositions of the individual, some form of adaptation takes place in which the individual attempts to arrive at a compromise between the institutional expectations and his own needs. We have called the individual's various attempts to effect such a compromise *adaptation* and can define it as the kind of behavior that affects the stability or equilibrium of either an individual or a social system. We have identified four modes of adaptation. Two are responses: *Activity* is when the individual teacher attempts to change the school's expectations to fit his own; *Passivity* is when an individual staff member adapts and changes his expectations to fit those of the school. The other two are attitudes: *Idealism* is the attitude that school improvement is a function of professional competence, shared policy making, and the personal feeling of control over educational improvement; and *Cynicism* is the attitude that the individual teacher has little power in determining educational policy and any improvements are dependent on administrative decisions. No matter what the mode, some form of adaptive behavior results when the individual find himself "stuck" in conflict situations between his own needs and the requirements of the organization.

Teachers in the sample were classified as to their mode of adaptation according to their score on the Teacher Interaction Style Questionnaire (TISQ).[6] The TISQ consisted of four scales measuring Activity–Passivity and Idealism–Cynicism. An example of an item from the Activity dimension is, "A person should start action toward modifying administrative policies in general disagreement with his own educational objectives." Teachers checked off whether they agreed strongly, moderately, or slightly, had no opinion, or disagreed slightly, moderately, or strongly.

Adaptation is the interaction between the response to conflict (Activity or Passivity) and the attitudes about the teacher's role (Idealism or Cynicism). This aspect of the study drew heavily on the work of McKelvey[7] who operationalized the concept of adaptation developed by Talcott Parsons.[8] The interaction of the four dimensions yields the following model:

	Activity	Passivity
Idealism	Crusading	Ritualism
Cynicism	Insurgency	Retreatism

FIGURE 3.1   THE McKELVEY MODEL

The terms "ritualism," "retreatism," "crusading," and "insurgency" were in part derived from the work of Robert Merton[9] and adapted by McKelvey. They are defined as follows:

> The *crusader*, or active idealist, is the individual (or faculty) who expresses confidence in the existing school structure but at the same time thinks it needs improvement and thus continually pushes to have ideas for improvement adopted within the school context. He is able to fulfill

the institutional expectations and his own personal need-dispositions with a minimum of strain, or what Getzels labels "integration."

The *ritualist,* or passive idealist, also likes the existing system and, although thinking it might be improved, conforms to the existing structure rather than "sticking his neck out" by pushing to have it changed. In other words, he has made the decision to conform to institutional expectations rather than express his own personal need-dispositions.

The *insurgent,* or active cynic, expresses opposition to the norms of the school in a negative, often hostile, manner and appears to be frustrated when his ideas for change are not adopted, maintaining that the only solution is to destroy the system and start all over again. He expresses his own needs over institutional expectations, which he rejects as personally irrelevant and meaningless.

The *retreatist,* or passive cynic, is in opposition to the school's norms and goals and expresses negative and hostile feelings toward the school and prefers to withdraw from attempting to influence the school by turning his attention elsewhere. He is in the school, but not of it. He rejects the fulfillment of both personal needs and institutional expectations while attempting to escape from all requirements and obligations. He is the "Mr. Nobody" in the school—apathetic, indifferent, and uninvolved—and is, indeed, in what Carlson has called "situational retirement."

ROLE–PERSONALITY CONFLICT, MODES OF ADAPTATION, AND ORGANIZATIONAL RENEWAL

Role–personality conflict and adaptation might certainly be found in an elementary school striving to achieve its goals. Some individuals in the school might object strenuously to a method of attaining this goal, while others might find it quite compatible with their own needs and expectations. Consequently, there could be individuals who react to a stated goal either by fighting it, attempting to change it, running away from it, ignoring it, adapting to it, or, in some cases, quitting the organization. In essence, some form of adaptive behavior results from commitment to the attainment of organizational goals. This is the nature of individual personalities interacting with the organization to which they belong. It is for this reason that the Getzels–Guba Model seemed applicable to the analysis of behavior in a given social system such as the elementary school. It provides researchers with the conceptual tools of analysis so that better understanding of the interactive process will result.

The general purpose of this study was to investigate how individuals adapt to work in an educational organization when there is discrepancy between institutional expectations and personal need dispositions. We attempted to describe role–personality conflict and the ways in which school people adapt to institutional demands. The central research question which guided the investigation can be stated in the following manner: *What is the relationship between role–personality conflict among school personnel and their modes of adaptation within schools committed to attaining a high level of organizational renewal?*

The significance of this study rests on the assumption that there are distinct differences in institutional–individual relationships which contribute to or detract from the ability of an organization to achieve its goals. The results of this study may provide a better understanding of role–personality conflict and the modes of adaptation occurring in high and low OR schools. In addition, these results contribute to the general body of research and knowledge in both the areas of social systems analysis and educational leadership.

Role–Personality Conflict and Modes of Adaptation

Our first task was to discover how role–personality conflict relates to modes of adaptation, and we asked, "Will an individual's role–personality conflict score have any relationship to his mode of adaptation?" We predicted that teachers with high role–personality conflict scores would have higher scores on the mode of adaptation dimensions of Passivity and Cynicism and lower scores on the dimensions of Activity and Idealism than would teachers who have low conflict scores.

As previously discussed, three different measures of role–personality conflict were obtained. Each of the three distributions of scores, which represented expectational, actual, and perceptual role–personality conflict for individual teachers from the eight sample schools, was divided into three groups. The high group for each of the three measures was composed of the upper quartile range of scores, the low group contained those scores in the lower quartile, and the scores between the upper and lower quartile comprised the middle group. Mean scores on the adaptation dimensions of Activity, Passivity, Idealism, and Cynicism for the high and low role–personality conflict groups were compared using a 1-tail t-test (see Glossary). Results of the analysis are presented in Table 3.1.

TABLE 3.1 COMPARISON OF HIGH AND LOW ROLE-PERSONALITY CONFLICT TEACHERS ON MODES OF ADAPTATION

Modes of Adaptation	High Conflict Group			Low Conflict Group			Mean₁ − Mean₂	t
	Mean₁	St. Dev.	N	Mean₂	St. Dev.	N		
A. Expectational Conflict								t (df = 80)
Activity	3.94	1.25	41	3.97	1.15	41	−.03	0.11
Passivity	4.58	1.15	41	4.29	1.33	41	.29	1.05
Idealism	4.40	1.26	41	4.54	1.09	41	−.14	0.53
Cynicism	4.56	1.13	41	4.06	1.00	41	.50	2.10*
B. Actual Conflict								t (df = 92)
Activity	3.83	1.30	48	4.20	1.20	46	−.37	1.42
Passivity	4.76	0.99	48	4.03	1.36	46	.73	2.96†
Idealism	4.34	1.16	48	4.55	1.03	46	−.21	0.92
Cynicism	4.30	1.12	48	4.02	1.14	46	.28	1.19
C. Perceptual Conflict								t (df = 77)
Activity	3.95	1.30	41	4.35	1.19	38	−.40	1.41
Passivity	4.65	1.10	41	3.90	1.32	38	.75	2.72†
Idealism	4.32	1.20	41	4.76	1.12	38	−.44	1.66
Cynicism	4.63	0.92	41	3.72	1.31	38	.91	3.55‡

* Significant .05
† Significant .01
‡ Significant .001

TABLE 3.2   FREQUENCY OF TEACHERS FROM HIGH AND LOW
ORGANIZATIONAL RENEWAL PROCESS SCHOOLS IN RELATION TO
ROLE–PERSONALITY CONFLICT

	High organizational renewal schools	Low organizational renewal schools	X^2
Expectational conflict			
High	10	32	
Low	34	9	23.81*
Actual role conflict			
High	15	35	
Low	34	15	13.82*
Perceptual role conflict			
High	12	35	
Low	23	15	9.23†

* Significant .001.
† Significant .01.

We found that teachers with high conflict scores tended to be more Passive and Cynical and teachers with low conflict scores tended to rank higher in Activity and Idealism. On the measure of expectational conflict, high conflict teachers were significantly higher on Cynicism than were low conflict teachers; in actual conflict, they were significantly higher in Passivity; and in perceptual conflict they were significantly higher on both Passivity and Cynicism. Though the differences between high and low conflict teachers was not significant on the other dimensions within each conflict category, the differences that did exist were in the predicted direction in all cases.

Role–Personality Conflict and OR

Our next question was, "Is there a relationship between the degree of role–personality conflict experienced by the teachers and the organizational renewal ranking of the school?" We hypothesized that low OR schools would have a greater number of teachers with high role–personality conflict than would high OR schools. To examine this question, teachers were assigned to a two-by-two frequency table on the basis of high or low conflict scores and high or low OR school membership, and a test of statistical significance (chi-square analysis; see Glossary) was carried out. Table 3.2 presents the results of this analysis. Our hypothesis was confirmed as on all three measures of conflict a significantly higher number of high conflict teachers was found in low OR schools than in high OR schools. This finding indicates that high role–personality conflict can indeed affect the degree of a school's success in attempting to develop dynamic processes which lead them to better attainment of their goals.

Modes of Adaptation and OR

We next turned our attention to establishing a relationship between the OR ranking of a school and the modes of adaptation of the teachers. The scores for all teachers in the high OR schools were compiled and the mean computed, and the same was done for the teachers in low OR schools. The mean scores for each group of teachers were compared on each of the adaptation dimensions and a t-test analysis was carried out to determine whether or not the differences between the means were significant. The results are presented in Table 3.3.

Our first hypothesis as to the relationship between OR and modes of adaptation was that high OR schools would have significantly higher scores on the Activity and Idealism modes of adaptation than low OR schools. This was confirmed. A significant difference was found on these dimensions between high and low OR schools.

The fact that the teachers in high OR schools had significantly higher scores on the Activity dimension suggests that they were taking more initiative and had more control over the interaction process than called for by their role expectations. Further, they were trying to change these expectations in the direction of greater agreement with their own perceptions. Higher scores on the Idealism dimension by

TABLE 3.3 COMPARISON OF SCHOOLS DEMONSTRATING HIGH AND LOW ORGANIZATIONAL RENEWAL PROCESSES ON MODES OF ADAPTATION

Modes of adaptation	Schools demonstrating high organizational renewal processes			Schools demonstrating low organizational renewal processes			$Mean_1 - Mean_2$	t (df = 189)
	$Mean_1$	St. Dev.	N	$Mean_2$	St. Dev.	N		
Activity	4.26	1.19	87	3.89	1.36	104	0.37	1.98*
Passivity	4.19	1.23	87	4.66	1.93	104	−0.47	1.94*
Idealism	4.71	1.07	87	4.42	1.12	104	0.29	1.79*
Cynicism	4.07	1.12	87	4.09	1.24	104	−0.02	0.14

* Significant .05 (1-tail test).

teachers in high OR schools indicates that these teachers express to a greater degree than low OR teachers the belief that school goals can be attained through professional competence, that teachers can take an active role in policy making in the school, and that they can have an influence on changes that are made.

We next predicted that low OR schools would have significantly higher scores on the Passivity and Cynicism modes of adaptation than high OR schools. From the t-test analysis presented in Table 3.3, it is apparent that there is a significant difference between the mean scores for the two groups of schools on Passivity but that there is no difference on the dimension of Cynicism. Higher scores for low OR schools on Passivity suggests that the teachers in these schools are more willing to modify and adjust their own educational beliefs in deference to administrative policy and existing conditions. Since the high and low OR schools did not differ on the mean scores for the Cynicism dimension, this may represent the expression of powerlessness the individual teacher feels when attempting to change things.

Figure 3.2 represents the composite findings for the four analyses discussed above. Further analyses were carried out to see if any predictions could be made as to degree of role–personality conflict or mode of adaptation on the basis of such demographic characteristics as teacher age, experience, length of time at present school, and so on. No significant differences were found for any of these factors.

INDIVIDUAL SCHOOL ANALYSES

It is also of importance to look at each of the schools on an individual basis and to describe the relationships which were found and some possible explanation of their existence. In order to compare across scales, school mean scores on the adaptation dimensions were converted to standard scores. In addition to the questionnaire data, supplementary information was obtained from interviews and observations which were not subjected to statistical tests, since the number of respondents was so small in each of the individual schools. Complete information about each of the schools may be found in Appendix A.

High Organizational Renewal Schools

Seastar As Figure 3.3 illustrates, role–personality conflict scores are lower than those of the other sample schools as compared to the League mean. They are also less active, passive, and cynical, but higher on idealism when compared to the League mean.

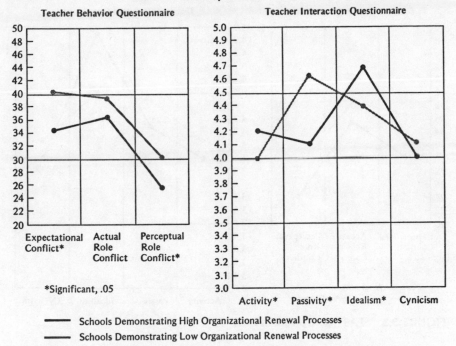

Teacher Behavior Questionnaire

Teacher Interaction Questionnaire

Expectational Conflict*   Actual Role Conflict   Perceptual Role Conflict*

*Significant, .05

Activity*   Passivity*   Idealism*   Cynicism

—— Schools Demonstrating High Organizational Renewal Processes

—— Schools Demonstrating Low Organizational Renewal Processes

FIGURE 3.2   COMPOSITE FINDINGS: ROLE–PERSONALITY CONFLICT AND MODES OF ADAPTATION IN SCHOOLS DEMONSTRATING HIGH AND LOW ORGANIZATIONAL RENEWAL PROCESSES

The lower score on Activity seems to be the result of a "leveling off" period, since early in the League project the school had adopted a flurry of changes and innovations. It may be that many of the teachers felt that their goals had already been achieved or else the school had declined in its attempt to improve, as the following quotes from Seastar indicate:

"I was really involved the first year, but my enthusiasm has died."
"We didn't get help when we needed it . . . we didn't want to stumble."
"It really sent me at first—but things got carried away; doing your own thing is bad."

However, most of the teachers seemed to feel the following quotes were illustrative of their school:

"The League has given teachers freedom to explore new teaching techniques without much restriction. . . ."
"It has set off a bomb in this school."

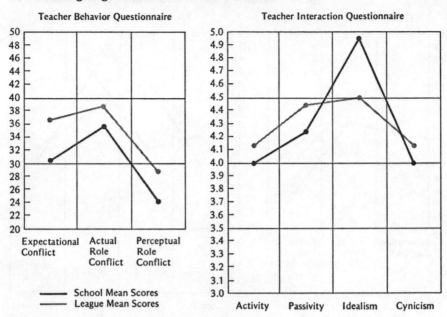

FIGURE 3.3 SEASTAR SUMMARY OF FINDINGS

While there may have been a "leveling off" within the school, there was certainly a great deal of positive sentiment for the goals and values of the school, as evidenced by the ranking on Idealism, which was the highest in the sample. Seastar seemed to enjoy excellent relationships with the community, between the teachers and the principal, and among the teachers themselves. The term "professionalism" was heard a great deal of the time from the staff, which seemed to take every opportunity to interact with one another either before school, at lunch, during recess, or after school. Their faculty meetings dealt with substantive issues and were jointly planned by principal and teachers. There were frequent discussions of school goals with spirited argument as to how best to implement them as a school staff. In addition, Seastar averaged only eight percent turnover of teachers over the period of the existence of the League, 1966–1970, compared with the League mean of twenty-one percent. In order to classify each school according to McKelvey's model, described above, the standard scores were compared on the Activity–Passivity dimensions and the Idealism–Cynicism dimensions. The higher score of each pair determined the classification. In the case of Seastar, the Activity score was somewhat higher than the Cynicism score, which serves to classify the school as crusading. Our observations indicated that the teachers were indeed highly motivated and self-directed and perhaps even underestimated their own efforts and capabilities in improving their school.

Shadyside As illustrated by Figure 3.4, Shadyside had the lowest scores on all three types of conflict when compared with the other seven schools in the sample. There were apparently few differences between the principal and his staff with regard to expectations for the teacher role in the school and the need-dispositions of the teachers. The following quotes are illustrative:

"Our faculty meetings are good dialogue sessions. There is lots of input from all the teachers. We don't feel inhibited. We sometimes meet in the classrooms of other teachers so that we can share ideas together."

"This is a very warm faculty. Most feel that they are in charge of the school."

"This faculty is a self-directed group—not much conflict."

"This principal allows teachers to try new ideas. He is very approachable. I feel that I can discuss ideas with him, and that they won't be held against me."

"We can't do 'our own things'—must work together."

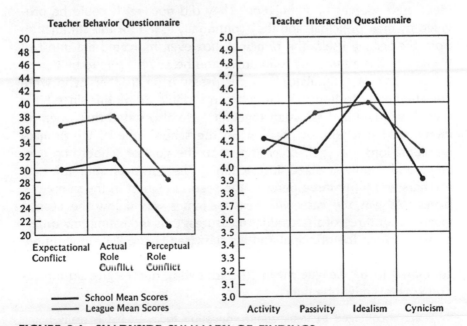

FIGURE 3.4   SHADYSIDE SUMMARY OF FINDINGS

The school also had scores on Activity and Idealism above the sample mean, with scores on Passivity and Cynicism well below the mean. The faculty as a group probably come closest to the typical crusader mode of adaptation. The one common criticism uncovered in the interviews was that of the principal and his leadership. For example:

"The principal is not persuasive. We need a stronger leader. We need more direction."

"I feel good about him now. He was weak a few months ago, but now he is taking a firm stand."

"I don't feel as confident or secure with a new principal. Wish he would take a stand—be more demanding."

Interestingly enough, only one teacher expressed dissatisfaction with the goals of the school:

"Yes, I have considered leaving school. My view is in the minority—yet, I don't want to be left out. But I still am frustrated. I find change a challenge, but I am hard to change. I am wary of it. I can't spread myself too thin—I am disturbed that there is not enough of me to go around."

In the interviews, the faculty kept indicating the need for new ideas, new sources of stimulation. They did not feel it could be provided by their principal, and they continually asked for this stimulation from the League itself. The principal, however, indicated that most of his faculty was attempting to improve and he saw his role to be that of a "prodder" or "stimulator," to put pressure on teachers who were not attempting to improve. He felt comfortable doing this since "it is a goal we identified as a staff together." He also stated that when he interviewed teachers for positions in the school, one of the primary considerations was their commitment to the goal of school improvement and "individualized instruction." The turnover rate for new teachers was thirty-three percent, the second highest in the sample.

James   As was the case with Seastar, James was below the League mean on all three of the conflict measures, thus indicating few differences between the principal and his staff (see Figure 3.5). In addition, they scored much higher on Activity and much lower on Passivity when compared to the League mean. The following quotes give an indication why this might be the case:

"We are encouraged to think about education today—what is really being taught."

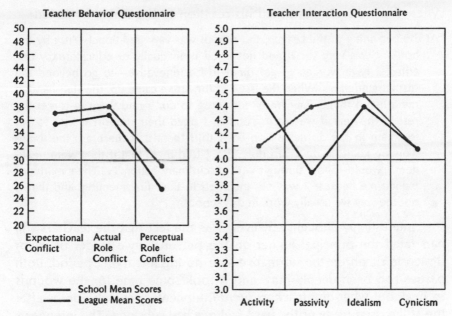

Teacher Behavior Questionnaire

Teacher Interaction Questionnaire

Expectational Conflict   Actual Role Conflict   Perceptual Role Conflict

——— School Mean Scores
——— League Mean Scores

Activity   Passivity   Idealism   Cynicism

FIGURE 3.5   JAMES SUMMARY OF FINDINGS

"Our principal expects us to try different things in our teaching, yet he
doesn't always expect success."

"He doesn't want to have to 'tell' you—he considers our needs and feelings."

"There isn't much direction provided—not many suggestions are offered as
to how to improve."

About half of the teachers in this school formed what they call the
"snoop group" which met regularly and had as one of its main purposes the encouragement of school improvement by intraschool classroom visitations and teacher evaluation by peers.

The lower scores on Idealism might be indicative of the situation
within the school district during the questionnaire phase of the study.
The teachers had threatened a one-day strike, and the principal of
James expressed his displeasure with the idea to the teachers. Many
of them resented his attitude and the interviews reflected upon some
of the reasons for their strong feelings:

"The principal is not the same since the strike—he was hurt by the faculty
reaction since he didn't expect us to vote for it. He lost enthusiasm for
us. It may be one reason why our communication isn't as good as last
year."

When the principal was asked his reaction to the strike, he stated:

"At the beginning of the League, this school was very traditional—'run by the book.' I was very social and not at all individually or educationally oriented. I have worked to get them to be innovative—to go beyond the district guidelines. When the issue of the strike came up, the staff handed me a list of things they were 'not going to do.' I told them to forget the rest of the year if we are in conflict. I need their support if I go to bat for them in the district office. So, I told them that these are the things 'you are going to do': yard duty, etc. I told them that if they were negligent I would follow through with disciplinary action. . . . Their militancy pained me because I was not included in their first meeting, and that is not the way we usually work in this school."

Interestingly enough, however, was the fact that the teachers still had rated the principal higher on the personal style leader behavior dimension than on the normative side during this trying period. Both parties had been deeply hurt, and it took some time for the wounds to heal, but when the teachers were interviewed several months after the strike issue many of the hard feelings had subsided. The interviews pointed out, however, the teachers' desire for the principal to improve his communication methods with the staff and their need for more praise and consideration from him on a more regular basis. Some teachers mentioned also that the "Hawthorne effect had worn out." Even though this may be the case, the teachers in James were for the most part highly motivated to improve their educational program, as the Activity score indicates. Only one teacher indicated a desire to leave because of dissatisfaction.

The school had thirty-one percent new teachers in the years 1966–1970. No reasons have been offered for the high rate, although some teachers did leave in the early years of the League due to disagreement with goals. The school is also part of a large urban school system, and turnover rates are traditionally high in that type of district. Based on the standard score comparison, the higher score on Cynicism in conjunction with the high score on Activity indicates that James School could be described as an example of the insurgent mode of adaptation.

Woodacres The findings from the Teacher Behavior Questionnaire and the Teacher Interaction Style Questionnaire for Woodacres are found in Figure 3.6. Woodacres was the only one of the high organizational renewal schools to rise above the League sample mean on one of the dimensions of conflict, that of expectational conflict. The teacher turnover figures for Woodacres were by far the highest in the sample, seventy percent over the four years of League participation. There was not a single teacher in the school at the time of data collection who had been there when the League began. The sixty-three percent turnover in the data collection year (seventeen new teachers in a staff of twenty-seven) is indicative of why there might have been conflict between what the principal expected of his teachers and what they perceived him to expect. This is particularly true since the questionnaires were administered after only two to three months on the job for many of the teachers. It is surprising, therefore, that the conflict scores were not even higher. One reason may be that all of the present staff members were hired by both the principal and the teachers in the school after lengthy interview sessions.

The teachers that had spent more than one year at Woodacres indicated some explanation as to why the Cynicism and Passivity scores were higher than might have been expected.

"Last year we had more discussions and meetings, but we don't discuss good ideas as much this year."

"Last year we were more openly 'gung-ho'—there was much more interac-

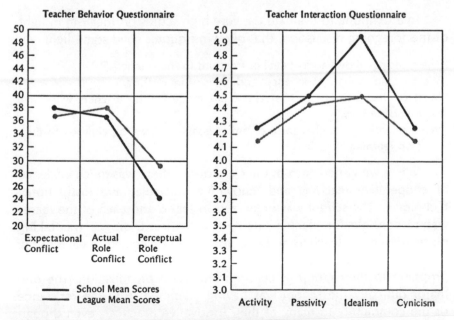

FIGURE 3.6   WOODACRES SUMMARY OF FINDINGS

tion among the staff with regard to goals—this year there are some hard feelings."

"The school is swinging more to the right—the reins are being tightened. There is more emphasis upon discipline and public relations due to community backlash over some of our programs."

The principal's view of this matter was:

"This is the first year I have really felt that I was in 'command' of the school since there were no longer any teachers here whom I had not hired. I always felt that I was living in the previous principal's shadow, particularly last year when one teacher always went directly to him with the problems of the school—she was a pipeline. . . ." (The previous principal had been promoted to the central office of the district.)

He also told us:

"Our goals are the same as they have been for the past one and one-half years, but we have not stressed them as much this year, particularly at the beginning of the year. We de-emphasized open structure and individualization at the start because of the high number of new teachers, even though we hired teachers who were tuned in to the goal of individualization . . . after the second month, we began to stress the goals again."

In attempting to evaluate the very high scores on Idealism in light of the foregoing discussion, the following quotes shed some light:

"The principal allows a great deal of freedom to the teachers."

"We are able to share experiences and ideas of innovating."

"Most of the decisions in this school are made by the teachers who have lots of leeway."

"We are working together for a common goal—committing children to their own learning."

When we visited each of the classrooms, there was much evidence of cooperative teaching and innovative curricular and instructional techniques. The school was organized in teams and each of the teams was responsible for planning its own activities. Dialogue was taking place among the teachers and decisions were delegated to each of the teams. In this way, each team could take the action they deemed appropriate to their group of children and team organization. The one major difficulty the school was having stemmed from the resistance of the community to many of their innovative practices, even though Woodacres had done more in attempting to dispel this resistance than any other school in the sample. Seminars were held with parents; questionnaires were sent home to obtain parental attitudes toward education; conferences were held with each parent having a child in the school, and numerous newsletters were sent home with the children. Many of the teachers, however, felt that there was too much "catering" to the parents and that the principal should take a firmer stand. This view did not predominate on the Woodacres faculty, however, since they gave their principal high marks on the personal side of the leader behavior ratings and indicated that he met their expectations for an ideal principal.

Low Organizational Renewal Schools

Fairfield Of all of the schools in the sample, Fairfield (see Figure 3.7) was found to have the highest conflict scores on both expectational and perceptual conflict and the second highest on actual role conflict. The principal expressed his expectations for the teacher role as follows:

"Teachers should accept more of the responsibility for the instructional program; I want them to change, even if in scissorlike steps. Teachers should

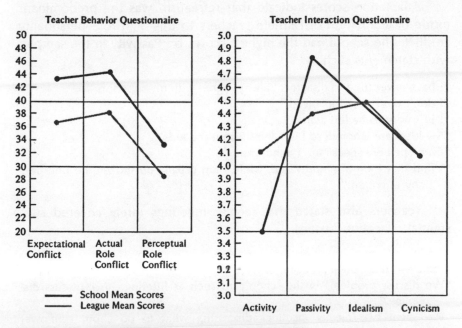

FIGURE 3.7 FAIRFIELD SUMMARY OF FINDINGS

have more decision making. The League is the finest thing that ever happened to me and the school. We needed the original input of ideas, but it has never really been implemented here."

The teachers, however, were not so sure of the value of innovation. Several identified a big split on the faculty between the "progressives" and the "traditionalists," with the former amounting to only twenty-five percent of the faculty and the latter accounting for about seventy-five percent. Some of the "traditionalists" stated:

"Too much change here is 'change for the sake of change.'"
"Good teachers don't have to team teach."
"Very few changes have been made here—this is a conservative group."
"The League has made me think more about change, but I haven't changed much myself. I am not negative—I just haven't made up my mind about it."

On the other hand, typical "progressive" comments were:

"Education must change. We aren't using horses and ice boxes anymore. The kids are thinking up in outer space, and we must teach them differently."
"The League has been good. I am enlightened by the discussions, and I try to imitate their ideas."

Adaptation scores indicate that retreatism was the predominant mode of adaptation of Fairfield teachers to this high role–personality conflict. The school had the highest scores on Passivity in the sample, with statements such as:

"I have never tried to disagree. I always agree with my superiors."
"I don't want to get involved."
"I just want to be left alone."
"My ideas are ignored, so I just think about the kids."
"Everyone here speaks up. I don't, though."
"I find that I am a minority and, while I am usually outspoken, no one pays any attention."

Teachers also stated that faculty meetings rarely covered substantial educational issues.

"Trivial and unimportant matters discussed."
"Principal 'runs' them . . . agendas rare."
"We discuss problems in the schoolyard such as littering. Also, discuss discipline."
"We spent two faculty meetings discussing what to do about sunflower seeds."
"We don't accomplish what we should. Every group needs a leader."

It is also interesting to note that Fairfield had the oldest faculty and a very low turnover rate among the teachers.

Perhaps the most striking finding from the interviews and observations was the teachers' very low regard for the student body, which was almost 100 percent minority. These attitudes may provide another explanation as to why the school ranks low in organizational renewal. Several of the teachers indicated feelings similar to the following:

"Too many kids here are not interested in learning. High absence rate. Low I.Q. Grades don't matter—they are only here in school because the law says so. Parents don't care. It has been hard to get any enthusiasm for learning. Thank heavens my own children aren't like these!"

"These minority kids just aren't verbal. They get away with too much. We need to be more strict. These kids just don't respect property. The children here can't be treated as individuals until they reach a certain age—they are just children."

When the teachers' attitudes toward their students are added to their passivity, it can be seen readily that this school has very far to go with respect to organizational renewal. The problem is further compounded by the fact that teachers identified a large discrepancy between the "ideal" and "real" dimensions on leader behavior and rated the principal very low on all six measures of the personal leader behavior dimensions. This, along with the high conflict, poor communications, and lack of initiative on the part of the teachers pose severe problems for this faculty and the leadership of the school.

Independence   Independence (see Figure 3.8) is the only low OR school scoring below the League mean on all three of the conflict measures. Their Activity score was just above the League mean, while scores on Passivity were among the highest in the total sample. Cynicism and Idealism were very close to the League mean scores.

For several years, the situation at Independence had made it very difficult for the faculty to work together on common goals and programs. The faculty, although serving under one principal, had been housed at two separate locations. The data collection year was the first time that they had been brought together. As a consequence, the questionnaires revealed a very high *esprit de corps* within the school and a great deal of talk about improvement and innovation. A typical teacher comment was: "It's nice to be in a big family again. Last year we were all mixed up in different school locations and double sessions."

However, during the interview phase, the school district was ordered to desegregate its schools and presented a plan by which In-

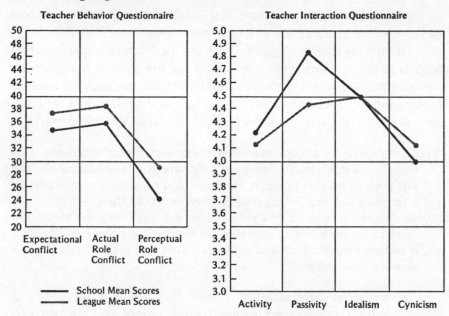

FIGURE 3.8   INDEPENDENCE SUMMARY OF FINDINGS

dependence would become a K-3 school in the next year. Consequently, the teachers were once again distressed over the future of
their school, not to mention their own job security. The principal
summed up the situation when he stated:

"This year was Camelot until the issue of desegregation came up. Previously,
we were on double sessions and the school was in complete turmoil.
Now, no one knows for sure where they will be next year."

The low scores on role–personality conflict for Independence are
indicative of the fact that communications had improved within the
school with regard to the expected teacher role in the school in comparison with the teachers' own statement of needs and wants. There
was some discontent, however, with what teachers felt they could do
as a group with respect to school improvement. Typical comments
were:

"I still teach the way I did before."
"I can get teaching materials and ideas on my own."
"This principal is not an inspiring leader. I know more than he does."
"I'm not sure what I'm doing."
"We need praise—he doesn't let us know when we are doing a good job."

The principal himself stated that he saw his role as that of a "facilitator" and that he wanted his teachers to be "open-minded and to try ideas." This, perhaps, offers one reason why this was the only low OR school to rate their principal high in the personal style of leader behavior. Several teachers also stated positive feelings about the changes taking place at the school.

"He wants us to work together to make it a better place for the child."
"Innovation is encouraged."
"We are all trying everything new."
"I chose to teach in this school to avoid a rut."

One of the more significant changes within the school was the attempt to improve the faculty meetings. The general faculty meetings had been considered a "waste of time." "The principal vents himself —feels like he has to 'control' the faculty," had been the general feeling. Under the new system, they were planned by a steering committee with time provided for team planning by breaking up into small groups.

Finally, the principal of Independence identified three different teacher reactions to the attainment of innovative goals:

"There are three groups of teachers on this faculty. The first is the 'avant-garde' group who are always seeking new ideas and ways to improve their teaching and the school; the second group is on the opposite end of the spectrum—they are traditional and resistant to new ideas; the third group consists of teachers in the middle—trying to improve in a limited way."

He further stated that many teachers had left the school because of their resistance to change and had gone on to other schools.

Independence, then, had shown overall improvement in its organizational renewal process, even though demonstrating a ritualistic mode of adaptation. It will be interesting to see how the desegregation plans affect the operation of the school in the future (see Chapter 5).
Bell Street As can be observed in Figure 3.9, Bell Street had very high scores on all three conflict measures when compared to the League sample mean, thus indicating wide disparities between the principal and teachers *vis-à-vis* expectations and needs. However, the mode of adaptation taken by the teachers to this conflict is very interesting. The scores on Activity and Cynicism were both quite high, thus putting the school in the mode of insurgent. The interviews were able to provide

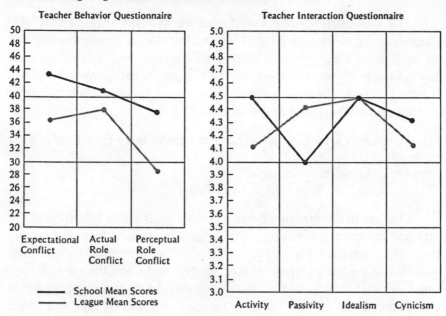

FIGURE 3.9   BELL STREET SUMMARY OF FINDINGS

some very valuable insights as to why the faculty responded in such a way to the high degree of conflict.

"The faculty here is not just putting in their time—they care about kids— it is not just a job."

"We all have varied backgrounds and different interests. It is a close faculty —a strong faculty—it is now performing leadership."

"Most of us feel the need for change."

"Teachers are given decision-making power with regard to school goals— we have lots of freedom to decide. We now have more discussions about education in the lunchroom—it is not just social."

The quotations illustrate the high degree of teacher activity and leadership exhibited in the school. Why then the high degree of conflict? Most of the teachers expressed negative sentiments toward the principal's leadership. The condemnations were perhaps the most severe in the entire sample:

"He is the 'Peter Principle' personified."

"He doesn't have the foggiest idea of what is happening here."

"I like him as a human being, but he could improve as an instructional leader."

"He is the type that wants your sympathy. Sometimes I feel we could get more done without a principal. We often want to protect him and, other times, punch him in the nose."

"There is a principal–teacher value conflict—the teachers turn to each other."

While the school tended more to Idealism than Cynicism, the faculty ranked number one among the sample schools with respect to their scores on the Cynicism dimension. For example:

"I have learned to play the [school district] 'game.' We teachers have our creativity shut up. Bell Street is a punishment for me. The administration are two-faced bastards. I have now become a yes-man—I just let fear govern me. I turn off my mind when I come here. I hang on just because they don't want me to. I stay in teaching because I love kids."

"We started working on the goal of improvement when the principal was absent from a faculty meeting."

It is worthwhile to note that even with the high degree of conflict between the principal and his teachers, the school was working hard to attain its goals.

Mar Villa Actual role–personality conflict scores for Mar Villa were lower than the League mean. However, scores for both expectational

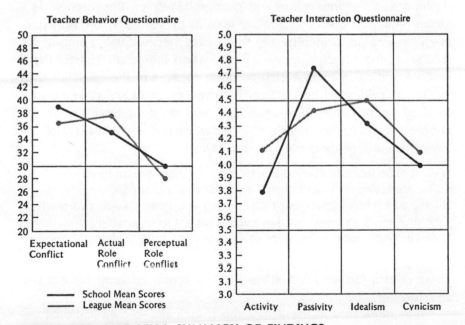

FIGURE 3.10 MAR VILLA SUMMARY OF FINDINGS

conflict and perceptual role–personality conflict were higher than the mean. Since these two measures are based on teachers' perceptions of the principal's expectations for them, it indicates that the principal was not adequately communicating his expectations to his staff. This was substantiated by the interviews:

"We don't get feedback on what we are doing."
"He doesn't give us pats on the back or appreciation."

In addition, the interviews were able to contrast the views of the principal and the teachers. The following were the principal's statements of his expectations for his teachers:

"Shape up and get on the ball; really begin to team teach; individualize instruction."

The teachers' perception of the principal's expectations were as follows:

"We could be anything we want to be, and he wouldn't care."
"Not clear."
"He doesn't care what our needs are."

The interviews and observations indicate that the principal was pushing hard for innovation and change. However, the teachers as a group tended to resist this goal, at least as presented by the principal. We were unable to identify any sign of teacher leadership among the faculty, as the ritualism mode of adaptation indicated. The principal was attempting to impose change upon them, and their reaction was apathy, as evidenced by the very high scores on Passivity. As may be recalled from Chapter 2, this principal was rated the lowest of all the sample schools on the relationship between real and ideal leader behavior. The following quotes are illustrative:

"I want to be treated as an individual—not as a piece of furniture."
"After expressing my ideas to him, I was told to get a transfer."
"In the past when I spoke out I could see I was getting a negative reaction. After you have been shut down you learn not to say anything."
"We all try to buck at first—try to discuss it or bring a different point of view—after a while you just go along."

These quotes further substantiate the low scores on both the Activity and Idealism dimensions.

It is interesting to note that the principal's sole educational experience had been in this school. He taught there and served as its principal for a total of seventeen years. He admitted that his greatest weakness was his inability to verbalize his thoughts. He frequently brought in outside consultants to present the ideas he valued with regard to change. The teachers referred to these consultants as his "hatchet men." Several teachers indicated that their dissatisfaction was so great that they were planning to leave at the end of the school year.

"You bet I'm leaving—he wants us to change, but he is not willing to himself."

"He is totally incapable of leadership. He never visits my classroom except to make criticism. He cannot communicate his ideas, so we never know where he stands. I don't think he would support the teachers if a problem came up."

The communications gap was further highlighted by the teachers' comments on their faculty meetings:

"There is very little dialogue."
"I am happy to get out of them."
"We used to have them 'when necessary.' Now we have them every Tuesday whether we need them or not."
"Businesslike, short, and to the point."

The principal's comments on the faculty meetings were also revealing:

"I try to average them every other week. We don't have nearly enough dialogue—some never talk. I can 'out-fox' them though. Since I am nonverbal, I am able to sit and wait and not talk until one of them will say, 'somebody say something!' "

Reflecting upon the statistical findings as well as the results of observations and interviews, it is easy to see why this school is having difficulty in attempting to achieve its goals—a high degree of role–personality conflict and a ritualistic adaptation mode by the teachers yields a "prototype model" of a low OR school.

CONCLUSIONS AND RECOMMENDATIONS

The results of this investigation demonstrate the utility of the Getzels model in identifying discrepancies between school expectations and individual needs, whether perceived or actual. It was an important outcome in addition to be able to classify schools, as well as individuals, on the basis of differences which existed between expectations and needs. The fact that these differences seemed to have an important impact upon the school's ability to attain its goals was a major finding in the study and appears to identify an important factor which can contribute to or detract from the improvement of educational programs in American schools.

Another important finding was the pinpointing of three distinct types of role–personality conflict: expectational, actual, and perceived. Researchers and others interested in "conflict management" will now be required to be more specific when dealing with such a general concept as "role–personality conflict," since each of the three types identified empirically here yielded different modes of adaptation on the part of the teachers. Each will therefore require different and more creative responses if the conflicts are to be overcome or at the very least minimized.

Interesting also was the fact that age, teaching experience, length of time in education or in the school, marital status, and other related demographic information pertaining to the educational background of the teacher had no apparent relationship to either the degree of conflict or modes of adaptation found in the schools. The generalizations, and even stereotypes, about younger or better-educated teachers being more "change oriented" did not seem to hold up, at least in this endeavor. In fact, some of the most "progressive" teachers had few additional units beyond certification and were well over the age of forty. Something had triggered their motivation to improve the status quo, and it was largely related to the dynamics of the social system in which they were operating. The "system" had in fact fostered and nurtured their growth and desire to improve, and it was quite unrelated to their age and training. The high organizational renewal schools were generally found to have individuals who cared enough about the goals and values of the school and felt enough sense of control and power to modify and improve them on a continuous basis.

Data from Individual Teachers and Principals

The data discussed in this chapter were gathered to test the significance of role–personality conflict and modes of adaptation in the social system of schools and their relationship to organizational renewal. Our conclusions can be summarized briefly as follows:

Relationship between role–personality conflict and modes of adaptation Teachers experiencing high *expectational role–personality con-*

flict between what they perceived to be the principal's expectations for the teachers' role in the school and what the principal actually identified as his own expectations tended to the adaptation mode of cynicism. This means that those teachers feel that they have little power or influence over the determination of educational policy and that the dominant role in such determinations depends upon the leadership and initiative of the principal. They have chosen not to involve themselves in such efforts, thus allowing their negative feelings about the goals and values of the school to erect a zone of indifference between themselves and the principal's expectations for their role. Only through more frequent and substantive dialogue can this barrier be minimized. Though their scores on the Passivity dimension were not significantly higher than other teachers', the scores nevertheless indicate that these teachers are approaching retreatism which is totally dysfunctional in a social system attempting to reach its goals. They simply are unaware of what is expected of them and don't make much effort to find out.

Teachers experiencing high *actual role–personality conflict* between what their principal stated as his expectations for the teachers' role and their own statements of need-dispositions tended toward the adaptation mode of passivity. In this situation the teachers chose to modify their own expectations and needs regarding policy making and school improvements to fit those of the school and thus took no initiative to narrow the discrepancy themselves. These teachers also had high scores on Cynicism, which, though not significant in a statistical sense, lead again toward a retreatist posture.

Teachers experiencing high *perceptual role–personality conflict* conformed precisely to the adaptation mode of retreatism, thus demonstrating in a most graphic way the usefulness of the McKelvey model in terms of deviant modes of adaptation. These teachers seem to be in disagreement with the goals and values of the school and express negative feelings with respect to their own ability to change the situation. Since this measure of conflict is based on what the teacher perceives the principal's expectations to be, it indicates the power of perception as a determinant of individual behavior in a social system.

The tendency of teachers experiencing all three types of role–personality conflict to adopt the retreatist mode of adaptation is unfortunately reinforced in education where traditionally, merely by closing their classroom doors, teachers can wall themselves off from the healthy and productive interactions which are vital to a school attempting to renew itself. The result is all too often organizational stagnation rather than organizational renewal!

Relationships between high and low organizational renewal schools and role–personality conflict   Schools ranking low in organizational renewal had significantly higher *expectational* role conflict than those schools which ranked high. The fact that low OR schools had significantly more teachers experiencing high expectational conflict again indicates the effect of poor interaction and communications within the social system of the school. No opportunity seems to exist for both principal and teachers to gain insights and understanding regarding the other's expectations.

While there were no statistical differences between high and low OR schools on the dimension of *actual* role conflict, there were nevertheless significantly more teachers experiencing such conflict in low OR schools, again reflecting upon some of the reasons why these schools might have been less successful in their attempts to renew themselves. Obviously there was a minimum of dialogue and discussion about what the teachers' role should be, and the lack of communication created many difficulties on the road to renewal.

Faulty perception again played a major role in the low OR schools. There was significantly higher *perceptual* role conflict in the low OR schools, and, in fact, the lower the school ranked in the OR process, the higher were the scores on perceptual role conflict. As also might be predicted, there were significantly more teachers expressing such conflict in the low OR schools, thus reinforcing the notion that perception is a powerful stimulant in influencing human behavior in a social system.

Relationship between high and low organizational renewal schools and modes of adaptation   High organizational renewal schools were found to have significantly higher scores on Activity and Idealism, indicating that the teachers in those schools express a high degree of confidence and agreement with the existing structure of the school, largely because they feel that they have had success in getting their ideas for school improvement adopted and that their voice is influential in shaping the goals of the school. Their ability to achieve renewal through dialogue, decision making, and action (the OR process) was achieved through initiative and self-actualization and without the strain of conflict between expectations and needs.

Low OR schools had significantly higher scores on Passivity, further illustrating the importance of individual initiative in attempting the process of renewal. Apathy and indifference are key variables in understanding the low OR ranking of these schools.

Data Analyzed by Individual School

When looking at the findings from individual schools, several important concepts emerge:

Organizational Stagnation   One of the most difficult periods in the life of an organization occurs when persons perceive that their goals have been achieved. A case in point is Seastar which appears to have leveled off after a furious and successful attempt to attain its goals. The principal and teachers had created a dynamic social system and now have to work even harder to insure its lasting qualities. New goals have to be jointly established by the principal and the teachers with the newly stated expectations and needs incorporated within the boundaries of their social system. Knowing when to "come about" is a significant process in educational change. If done at the right time, the so-called "Hawthorne Effect" can be put to productive and effective use.

Transiency   The durability of a dynamic social system often may be of a "here today, gone tomorrow" variety. Change brought about by a threatened strike by the teaching staff at James or the return to a single school building at Independence are indicative of the delicate balance of a school's social system. It is very difficult to be different and deviate from traditional and well-entrenched norms of behavior, as many of the League schools were attempting to do. This ferment was occurring over a five-year period and there were frequent challenges to those schools attempting to develop a process of renewal.

Dissonance   L'Estrange once said that "that which is agreeable to the nature of one thing, is many times contrary to the nature of another." It was at Fairfield that we first uncovered the various splits on faculties which have to be reconciled if changes in the educational system are to become effective. The "traditionalists" were labeled as status quo and said that too much change there was "change for the sake of change." Another group identified at Fairfield was labeled the "progressives" (avant-garde at Independence), and it was their feeling that education had to change: "We aren't using horses and iceboxes anymore. The kids are thinking up in outer space, and we must teach them differently." Interviews with teachers in other schools uncovered a third group which might be appropriately labeled "the swing group," since they took the middle ground and shifted their loyalties between the progressives and the traditionalists, depending upon the issue at hand. The challenge to educational administration is in the reconciling and mediating of these disparate groups to the extent that they are able to work together toward a common goal.

Returning to Normalcy   The campaign slogan of Warren Harding, "return to normalcy," may also apply to education. Woodacres School decided to do just that after a sixty-three percent staff turnover brought seventeen new teachers to the school. It was the only high OR school to rise above the League mean on "expectational conflict" between the principal and the teachers. As one teacher indicated, "The school is swinging more to the right—the reins are being tightened." The principal, however, indicated that, while the goals of the school were the same that year as in the past, it took time to "tune in" the new teachers, and he therefore was slowing down the progress of change until the total staff could learn to work together toward a common goal.

In summary, then, stagnation, transiency, dissonance, and returning to normalcy are important concepts emerging from this study of the school as a social system. It is hoped that their relationship to the mediation of expectations and needs has been made evident in the foregoing discussion. It now seems appropriate to look at the influence of values on the same social systems.

NOTES

1   Chris Argyris, *Personality and Organization*, Harper and Row, New York, 1957.

2   Jacob Getzels, James M. Lipham, and Roald F. Campbell, *Educational Administration as a Social Process: Theory, Research, Practice*, Harper and Row, 1968.

3   Melvin Seeman, "Role Conflict and Ambivalence in Leadership," *American Sociological Review*, vol. 18, August 1953, pp. 373–380. For a significant related approach, see Neal Gross, Ward Mason, and Alexander W. McEachern, *Explorations in Role Analysis: Studies of the School Superintendency Role*, John Wiley & Sons, New York, 1958.

4   Samuel A. Stouffer, "An Analysis of Conflicting Social Norms," *American Sociological Review*, vol. 14, December 1949, pp. 707–717.

5   Merton Campbell, "Self-Role Conflict Among Teachers and Its Relationship to Satisfaction, Effectiveness, and Confidence in Leadership." Unpublished doctoral dissertation, University of Chicago, 1958.

6   William W. McKelvey, "Expectational Non-Complementarity and Deviant Adaptation in a Research Organization." Unpublished doctoral dissertation, Massachusetts Institute of Technology, 1967.

7   Ibid.

8   Talcott Parsons, *The Social System*, The Free Press, Glencoe, Illinois, 1951, p. 250.

9   Robert K. Merton, "Social Structure and Anomie," *Social Theory and Social Structure*, 1968, pp. 185–214.

CHAPTER 4
VALUES OF PARENTS, TEACHERS, AND PRINCIPALS

J. W. Getzels' theoretical model for studying the school as a social system includes three major dimensions: the nomothetic, the idiographic, and the cultural.[1] The nomothetic deals with the needs and expectations that the institution has in order to attain its prescribed goals. The idiographic deals with the needs and expectations of the individuals who work in the institution. The cultural dimension encircles both the nomothetic and idiographic dimensions, since the institution is part of some larger culture and the individuals who work in that institution have themselves come from some particular culture.

Since the mid-1950s when Getzels and Guba first put together the model, many researchers have studied the relationship between the nomothetic and the idiographic dimensions of the model; too little attention, unfortunately, has been given to the relationship of the cultural dimension to both the nomothetic and the idiographic dimensions. As Getzels says, "The expectations for behavior in given institutions not only derive from the requirements of the social system of which the institution is a part but also are related to the values of the culture which is the context for the particular social system."[2] For example, within the educational context, driver education may not be an important part of the curriculum in a community which stresses preparation for university work, and foreign language may not be an important part of the curriculum in a community which stresses vocational training.

Getzels believes there are two types of American values—sacred and secular. The sacred values are part of the American "creed" and constitute our basic (and undivorceable) beliefs. Democracy, individualism, equality, and human perfectability are the four sacred values

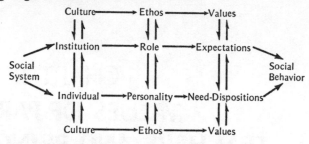

FIGURE 4.1   THE GETZELS MODEL

of our society. However, in addition to these, there is a core of working beliefs which constitute our secular values. These secular values were identified and described first by social scientist George D. Spindler, who influenced Getzels' concepts and ideas of values. Spindler feels that our society is undergoing a fundamental shift in secular values.

> I believe American Culture is undergoing a transformation, and a rapid one producing many disjunctions and conflicts, from the traditional to the emergent value systems. . . . But recently, and under the impetus of World Wars, atomic insecurities, and a past history of boom and bust, the heretofore latent tendencies in the emergent direction have gathered strength and appear to be on the way towards becoming the dominant value system of American Culture.[3]

Similar to David Riesman's *The Lonely Crowd* and his dichotomy of inner-directed and other-directed individuals, Spindler's dichotomy revolves around secular values that he refers to as traditional and emergent. He categorizes the components of each as follows:[4]

Traditional Values	Emergent Values
Puritan morality (Respectability, thrift, self-denial, sexual constraint; a Puritan is someone who can have anything he wants, as long as he does not enjoy it!)	**Sociability** (One should like people and get along well with them. Suspicion of solitary activities is characteristic.)
Work-success ethic (Successful people worked hard to become so. Anyone can get to the top if he tries hard enough. So people who are not successful are lazy, or stupid, or both. People must work desperately and	**Relativistic moral attitude** (Absolutes in right and wrong are questionable. Morality is what the group thinks is right. Shame-, rather than guilt-oriented personality, is appropriate.)

Traditional Values	Emergent Values
continuously to convince themselves of their worth.)	
Individualism (The individual is sacred, and always more important than the group. In one extreme form, the value sanctions egocentricity, expediency, and disregard for other people's rights. In its healthier form the value sanctions independence and originality.)	**Consideration for others** (Everything one does should be done with regard for others and their feelings. The individual has a built-in radar that alerts him to others' feelings. Tolerance for the other person's point of view and behaviors is regarded as desirable, so long as the harmony of the group is not disrupted.)
Achievement orientation (Success is a constant goal. There is no resting on past glories. If one makes $9,000 this year, he must make $10,000 next year. Coupled with the work-success ethic, this value keeps people moving, and tense.)	**Hedonistic, present-time orientation** (No one can tell what the future will hold; therefore, one should enjoy the present—but within the limits of the well-rounded, balanced personality and group.)
Future-time orientation (The future, not the past, or even the present, is most important. There is a "pot of gold at the end of the rainbow." Time is valuable and cannot be wasted. Present needs must be denied for satisfactions to be gained in the future.)	**Conformity to the group** (Implied in the other emergent values. Everything is relative to the group. Group harmony is the ultimate goal. Leadership consists of group-machinery lubrication.)

In order to visualize the conflicts that arise out of a difference in values between the school and its surrounding culture, Spindler created a continuum from traditional to emergent values and placed the different groups operating in the context of relations between school and community in different positions on the continuum. He postulated the varying degrees and mixtures of traditional and emergent orientations of these groups as follows:[5]

Traditional Values			Emergent Values
			(younger)
public and parents	administrators		students
school boards	students (older)	teachers (older)	teachers (younger)

FIGURE 4.2   SPINDLER'S TRADITIONAL AND EMERGENT CONTINUUM

Spindler placed school boards nearest the traditional end of the continuum because these boards are usually composed of persons representing the powerful, status quo elements of the community who, by virtue of their age, acquired their value sets during a period of time when American culture was more tradition-oriented than it is today. The public tends to be more traditional than professional educators, complaining that their children are not being taught the "three R's," that educators want to "socialize" the competitive system by eliminating report cards, that children are not taught the meaning of hard work. Students are placed at two points on the continuum because those coming from traditionalist family environments will tend to hold traditionalist values, though less securely than their parents did. Other students who come from emergent-oriented families will tend to place even further toward the emergent end of the line than their parents. Older teachers will tend to hold relatively traditionalist views by virtue of their age, and younger teachers will be more emergent-oriented since they acquired their personal culture during a relatively more emergent-oriented period of American history. Because the school administrator must face many traditional people in his job performance, he tends to be more traditional than his teachers.

Spindler sees a difference in values as the root of conflict in social and institutional settings:

> The traditionalist views the emergentist as "socialistic," "communistic," "spineless and weak-headed," or downright "immoral." The emergentist regards the traditionalist as "hidebound," "reactionary," "selfish," or "neurotically compulsive." Most of what representatives of either viewpoint do may be regarded as insidious and destructive from the point of view of the other. The conflict goes beyond groups or institutions, because individuals in our traditional society are likely to hold elements of both value systems concomitantly. There are few "pure" types. The social character of most is split, calling for different responses in different situations, and with respect to different symbols. So an ingredient of personal confusion is added that intensifies social and institutional conflict.[6]

Data Collection from Parents

A major difference between this study and those reported in Chapters 2 and 3 was that the questions we were asking about the effect of culture and values on the social system of the school required gathering data from parents as well as from teachers and principals. Additional data-gathering procedures were therefore required to supplement the procedures reported earlier.

In each of the eight schools, random numbers were used to select the names of thirty families in the community. Three alternates were also chosen for each school in case any families moved during the study. In order to check the ethnic representativeness of the sample taken for each school, a comparison was made between ethnic grouping percentages of the school community as a whole gathered by district survey and the random sample we had drawn. The families selected to participate in this study were within one to two percentage points of the ethnic breakdown determined by the district survey. The percentage of ethnic groups in the populations of the eight sample schools is shown in Table 4.1.

TABLE 4.1 PERCENTAGE OF ETHNIC GROUPS IN THE EIGHT SAMPLE SCHOOLS

| School name | School district survey results | | | | |
	Spanish	Other white	Oriental	Black	Other
Seastar	7	79	13	0	1
Shadyside	18	78	1	2	1
James	4	73	2	17	4
Woodacres	1	99	0	0	0
Fairfield	78	2	11	9	0
Independence	24	64	3	6	3
Bell Street	35	25	10	30	0
Mar Villa	41	53	1	5	0

The following procedure for collecting data from parents was used in all schools except Fairfield. Parents were first contacted by phone and then the questionnaires were mailed. Ten days later, all thirty parents were phoned again to determine if they had completed the questionnaire. A final call was made to those families that had said the previous time that they had not mailed in their questionnaires.

In Fairfield, the majority of families spoke only Spanish and had no telephones. Therefore, personal visits were made to each of the thirty families to tell them about the purpose of the study. The school secretary, who spoke fluent Spanish, went along on these visits.

In the eight schools plus the pilot school, there were 270 possible respondents; by using the procedures described above, 247 questionnaires (ninety-two percent response) were received in usable form.

Values of Parents, Teachers, and Principals

The purpose of this study was to examine the effect of the cultural dimension on the social system of the school. We felt that by examining the value orientations of the parents, teachers, and principals and the congruencies or incongruencies among them we could better understand the social system of the school and its ability to achieve its goals.

Our first task, then, was to discover and identify the differences in values among parents, teachers, and principals. In accordance with Spindler's continuum, we predicted that parents would be the most traditional, followed by principals and then by teachers. The values defined as *traditional* were work-success ethic and achievement orientation, future-time orientation, individualism, and Puritan morality. *Emergent* values were the ethic of sociability and consideration for others, present-time orientation, group conformity, and relative morality. Explanations of these values may be found in the chart from Spindler's work presented above.

The Differential Values Inventory (DVI)[7] was used to measure the values of the community, teachers, and principal. The instrument consists of sixty-four pairs of statements such as:

A. Enjoy myself doing things with others.
B. Enjoy myself doing many things alone.

or

A. Say what I think is right about things.
B. Think of the effect on others before I speak.

The directions ask the respondent to preface each statement with "I ought to . . ." and to select the statement with which he most agrees. Respondents are required to make a choice on all items.

In order to make the forced choice between statements more palatable, respondents were given the option of checking either "This choice was difficult for me to make" or "This choice was easy for me to make" for each item. This has two advantages. First, it relieved some of the discomfort of the respondents caused by the instrument's format, which forced them to choose only one statement for each item, even when they might believe that both statements or neither reflect what they felt they ought to do. Also, this addition doubled the number of items in the instrument and so helped to give a greater dispersion on the final scores.

Minor revision in the instrument was necessitated by the fact that the instrument had been designed for use with administrators, teachers, and students. Therefore, some wording had to be changed to make it appropriate also for parents. For example, "Work harder than most of those in my class" was changed to "Work harder than most of those in my job." Since the meaning of the statement was unchanged, this wording was used for principals and teachers as well as for parents.

The second revision of the Differential Values Inventory made for this study was to have the questionnaire translated into Spanish. In five of the eight communities, there were enough Spanish-speaking families to warrant this change.

The data gathered by the DVI were subjected to a 2-tail t-test (see Glossary) to see if significant differences could be found among the values expressed by parents, teachers, and principals. Significant differences were found between and among all three. Tables 4.2, 4.3, and 4.4 illustrate the differences for these groups on the eight value dimensions.

Parents and Principals   Parents and principals differed significantly on each of the eight dimensions. In addition, parents scored higher on the four traditional value dimensions, and principals scored higher on the four emergent value dimensions. We could thus confirm that parents have more traditional values than principals, as Spindler predicted.

Parents and Teachers   Parents and teachers also differed significantly on all eight dimensions. Parents scored significantly higher than teachers on all four traditional value dimensions, while teachers were significantly higher than parents on the emergent dimensions. Again, we support Spindler by confirming that parents tend to have more traditional values than teachers.

Principals and Teachers   Our findings were not in accord with Spindler's model when the value orientations of teachers and principals were compared. Spindler had predicted that teachers would be more emergent than principals, but we found that principals scored significantly higher than teachers on the four emergent values. Teachers' scores were significantly higher than principals' on the traditional values Work-Success and Individualism. Their scores on Puritan Morality and Future-Time Orientation were also higher than those of the principals, though the differences between the two groups on these dimensions were not significant.

TABLE 4.2 A COMPARISON OF PRINCIPALS' VALUES AND PARENTS' VALUES IN THE EIGHT SAMPLE SCHOOLS

	Values	Principals		Parents		Mean₁ − Mean₂	t	Probability <
		Mean$_1$	St. Dev.	Mean$_2$	St. Dev.			
Traditional	Work-Success (and Achievement Orientation)	6.89	3.55	14.46	1.37	7.57	5.63	.001
	Puritan Morality	7.00	2.78	14.92	1.89	7.92	6.66	.001
	Individualism	11.56	2.96	17.38	0.94	5.82	5.30	.001
	Future Time	7.22	4.38	16.77	1.73	9.55	5.74	.001
Emergent	Sociability (and Consideration for Others)	24.89	4.81	12.08	0.98	12.81	7.38	.001
	Relative Morality	26.67	4.12	16.77	1.43	9.90	6.42	.001
	Conformity	11.89	2.71	7.47	1.00	3.42	4.33	.001
	Present Time	22.44	4.85	14.14	1.27	12.30	4.68	.001

TABLE 4.3   A COMPARISON OF TEACHERS' VALUES AND PARENTS'
VALUES IN THE EIGHT SAMPLE SCHOOLS

	Values	Teachers		Parents		Mean₁ − Mean₂	t	Probability ≤
		$Mean_1$	St. Dev.	$Mean_2$	St. Dev.			
Traditional	Work-Success (and Achievement Orientation)	10.28	1.23	14.46	1.37	4.18	6.42	.001
	Puritan Morality	8.59	1.33	14.92	1.89	6.33	7.75	.001
	Individualism	15.57	0.70	17.38	0.94	1.81	4.37	.001
	Future Time	10.29	1.11	16.77	1.73	6.48	8.92	.001
Emergent	Sociability (and Consideration for Others)	18.33	0.85	12.08	0.98	6.25	13.63	.001
	Relative Morality	22.57	1.22	16.77	1.43	5.80	8.73	.001
	Conformity	9.58	1.26	7.47	1.00	2.11	3.71	.01
	Present Time	17.66	1.40	14.14	1.27	3.52	5.27	.001

TABLE 4.4 A COMPARISON OF TEACHERS' VALUES AND PRINCIPALS' VALUES IN THE EIGHT SAMPLE SCHOOLS

	Values	Teachers		Principals		$Mean_1 - Mean_2$	t	Probability $\geq$
		$Mean_1$	St. Dev.	$Mean_2$	St. Dev.			
Traditional	Work-Success (and Achievement Orientation)	10.28	1.23	6.89	3.55	3.39	2.55	.05
	Puritan Morality	8.59	1.33	7.00	2.78	1.59	1.46	—
	Individualism	15.57	0.70	11.56	2.96	4.01	3.73	.01
	Future Time	10.29	1.11	7.22	4.38	3.07	1.92	—
Emergent	Sociability (and Consideration for Others)	18.33	0.85	24.89	4.81	6.59	3.80	.01
	Relative Morality	22.57	1.22	26.67	4.12	4.10	2.70	.05
	Conformity	9.58	1.26	11.89	2.71	2.31	2.19	.05
	Present Time	17.66	1.40	22.44	4.85	4.78	2.68	.05

Congruency of Values and OR Ranking

Our next question concerned the relationship between the congruency or lack of congruency of values between the school and the community and the organizational renewal ranking of the school. We predicted that we would find a greater agreement about values among parents, teachers, and principals in high OR schools than we would in low OR schools.

The results of the Mann-Whitney U test (see Glossary) indicated that our hunch was not correct. We found no significant differences between high and low OR schools when we looked at congruence of values. In other words, the differences in values between teachers and principals, between teachers and parents, and between principals and parents were not significantly smaller in high OR schools than they were in low OR schools.

Relationship of Values to Other Variables

We were interested to see whether any of the following variables were highly correlated with traditional–emergent values of teachers and parents: age, education, family income, and number of organizations (professional and nonprofessional) to which teachers and parents belong. As indicated in Chapters 2 and 3, we had asked teachers to fill out a biographical questionnaire to gather this demographic data. In order to obtain similar data from the parents, a set of biographical questions was included on the final page of the parents' copy of the Differential Values Inventory. These items were not placed on the first page since some individuals, seeing personal questions, might conclude that the entire questionnaire was also personal in nature and might be discouraged from returning it to the school. By placing these questions on the last page, we hoped that most parents would fill out the entire questionnaire and, if not willing to complete the biographical items, would at least return the Differential Values Inventory without the last page.

We found no significant relationships between these four demographic items and teacher–parent values. We feel that this result is quite important, since it is frequently conjectured among educators that age or education has a direct bearing upon one's value orientation. Data collected in this study do not support this common belief. Table 4.5 presents comparative statistics that support this statement.

TABLE 4.5 A COMPARISON OF DEMOGRAPHIC DATA FOR TEACHERS
AND PARENTS IN THE EIGHT SAMPLE SCHOOLS

School Name	Age		Highest Grade Level Attained		Family Income		Number of Organizations	
	Teachers	Parents	Teachers	Parents	Teachers	Parents	Teachers	Parents
Seastar	42.4	35.6	17.3	12.7	19,981 (11,694)*	12,130	3.9	1.9
Shadyside	32.3	33.5	16.6	11.4	14,723 (8,915)	9,734	2.9	1.0
James	35.6	32.4	17.0	11.8	16,698 (9,745)	7,450	2.6	2.0
Woodacres	31.2	32.8	16.7	13.2	16,045 (8,165)	13,365	2.2	1.9
Fairfield	43.7	37.5	16.8	10.2	11,656 (8,554)	4,553	2.5	1.5
Independence	40.1	36.4	17.0	12.0	18,480 (10,103)	9,708	2.8	1.5
Bell Street	36.1	36.2	16.6	11.5	17,230 (10,329)	11,026	2.3	1.1
Mar Villa	38.7	36.8	16.7	11.0	15,190 (10,793)	7,250	3.2	1.5

* Income from teaching (excludes other family income).

The biographical questionnaire also asked teachers and parents to indicate the number of contacts they had with one another through telephone calls, letters, and personal visits. These data were collected to determine whether there was any difference in the amount of communication between teachers and parents in the high OR schools and the low OR schools. Again, no significant differences were found.

Table 4.6 compares the type and amount of contact the teachers and parents had in each of the sample schools. The table should be read so that the reader judges the communication process as a complete cycle. For example, the first cycle is the number of calls parents made to teachers and the number of calls teachers made to parents. The intent of the table is to point out discrepancies in the perceptions

TABLE 4.6 TYPE AND AMOUNT OF COMMUNICATION BETWEEN TEACHERS AND PARENTS FOR THE EIGHT SAMPLE SCHOOLS

Types of Communication	Schools							
	Sea-star	Shady-side	James	Wood-acres	Fair-field	Inde-pendence	Bell	Mar Villa
Number of calls from parents (teachers)	12.0	18.9	10.0	20.0	1.6	14.5	3.9	12.8
Number of calls to teachers (parents)	5.5	1.0	2.7	1.7	5.5	2.2	2.0	3.7
Number of calls to parents (teachers)	21.6	24.2	19.0	33.8	3.8	17.2	13.7	16.8
Number of calls from teachers (parents)	6.2	1.3	3.4	2.8	4.3	2.7	1.7	2.2
Number of letters from parents (teachers)	10.7	14.5	6.7	12.2	1.2	19.6	6.0	16.8
Number of letters to teachers (parents)	2.5	1.0	2.7	1.3	NA*	2.6	1.2	2.3
Number of letters to parents (teachers)	20.2	19.8	15.1	19.4	1.7	17.8	22.5	20.0
Number of letters from teachers (parents)	2.3	2.3	3.0	1.7	NA	1.8	1.9	1.2
Number of visits from parents (teachers)	22.5	13.2	26.7	25.4	11.3	23.3	17.4	19.5
Number of visits to teachers (parents)	3.0	3.5	6.5	4.2	3.1	2.3	1.5	3.0
Number of visits to parents (teachers)	4.0	8.4	15.1	8.9	4.9	6.6	3.8	11.3
Number of visits from teachers (parents)	3.3	2.5	2.3	0.6	1.4	1.3	1.3	1.5

* NA = Data not available.

of parents and teachers, for example, between the number of calls from parents that teachers say they receive and the number of calls that parents say they make to teachers. Note that in all schools teachers specified that they had more contact with parents than parents specified they had with teachers.

INDIVIDUAL SCHOOL PROFILES

The following section reports on the interviews which were held in each of the eight schools. Although many questions were asked of the teachers interviewed, only the answers to one question are reported here: Is there a difference of values between the community and the school?

Tables 4.7 through 4.14 present the mean scores in each school for teachers and parents and the principal's scores on each dimension. T-tests were used to ascertain significant differences on value dimensions between teachers and parents, but since the principal's score represents only one individual rather than a group, his score is reported for comparison purposes without statistical analysis. For purposes of reporting the subjective data, we treat the school—principal and teachers—as a single unit. In conjunction with each table, the subjective data for that school are reported which support or contradict the objective data in the school. The teachers' answers which are reported are representative of all the teachers who were interviewed in that school.

High Organizational Renewal Schools

Seastar   The DVI indicated that teachers and parents had significantly different means on four of the value dimensions (see Table 4.7). The parents scored significantly higher on the traditional values Puritan Morality and Future-Time Orientation, while teachers were significantly higher on the emergent values Sociability and Relative Morality. In the only departure from what would be predicted by the Spindler continuum, parents scored slightly, though not significantly, higher on the emergent value of group conformity. However, the interviews revealed that the teachers did not perceive any difference in values between parents and faculty. The following are representative statements made by the faculty: "Although the parents do not always agree with

TABLE 4.7 A COMPARISON OF THE PRINCIPAL, TEACHERS, AND PARENTS IN SEASTAR ELEMENTARY SCHOOL (WEIGHTED SCORE MEANS)

	Values	Principal	Teachers (n = 21)		Parents (n = 29)		$\text{Mean}_1 - \text{Mean}_2$	t	Probability $\leq$
			Mean_1	St. Dev.	Mean_2	St. Dev.			
Traditional	Work-Success (and Achievement Orientation)	8.00	10.62	5.36	11.72	5.58	−1.10	0.69	—
	Puritan Morality	7.00	7.86	3.34	12.14	5.40	−4.28	3.15	.01
	Individualism	17.00	16.10	4.24	16.59	4.32	−0.49	0.39	—
	Future Time	10.00	9.81	5.43	13.97	5.70	−4.16	2.54	.05
Emergent	Sociability (and Consideration for Others)	25.00	18.38	4.87	14.10	5.08	4.28	2.93	.01
	Relative Morality	26.00	23.57	4.84	18.83	5.06	4.74	3.26	.01
	Conformity	14.00	8.29	3.58	9.21	4.30	−0.92	0.78	—
	Present Time	18.00	17.57	3.84	16.55	4.90	1.02	0.78	—

the teachers, there is no real value conflict"; "There is no difference of values between the parents and the teachers"; "The parents like the learning center in the school. There is no community resistance." Seastar's success in achieving its goals and its excellent relations with its community are reflected in these comments.

Shadyside   Shadyside fits our expectations as the parents were shown to have more traditional values than teachers. Teachers scored significantly higher than parents on all four emergent values. Parents' scores were higher on all traditional values, and only for the Individualism dimension was the difference not statistically significant (see Table 4.8). The interviews revealed that some teachers believed that parents had different values than themselves; however, other teachers indicated that they did not perceive any value differences between teachers and parents. The following are representative statements made by the faculty:

"I believe some parents complain, but generally there is no value conflict between the community and the teachers."

"I believe that the community does not have a different set of values than the faculty. However, parents want schools to teach what is measurable; the home will teach what is unmeasurable."

"I do not know the community very well. However, politically, the parents are probably very conservative, and this faculty would be very liberal."

Perhaps most revealing is this teacher comment: "The parents do not have a different set of values; however, when I talk to parents, I always stress that academic subjects are being taught in school." She obviously senses the more traditional "academic" orientation of the parents.

James   The DVI indicated that teachers and parents had significantly different values on all eight dimensions (Table 4.9), and all dimensions fit the expectations of the Spindler continuum.

In the interviews, some teachers specified that there were no value differences between parents and faculty. Others, however, did perceive a difference of values. The following are representative statements made by the faculty:

"There are two factions in the community. The first faction is made up of permanent families. These families have retired from the military. They

TABLE 4.8 A COMPARISON OF THE PRINCIPAL, TEACHERS, AND PARENTS IN SHADYSIDE ELEMENTARY SCHOOL (WEIGHTED SCORE MEANS)

	Values	Principal	Teachers (n = 22)		Parents (n = 29)		Mean₁ − Mean₂	t	Prob-ability ≤
			Mean₁	St. Dev.	Mean₂	St. Dev.			
Traditional	Work-Success (and Achievement Orientation)	3.00	9.73	5.21	14.86	6.96	−5.14	2.84	.01
	Puritan Morality	4.00	6.73	3.99	15.38	4.95	−8.65	6.58	.001
	Individualism	9.00	15.64	4.10	16.62	3.78	−0.98	0.87	—
	Future Time	4.00	9.68	5.06	17.45	7.56	−7.77	4.08	.001
Emergent	Sociability (and Consideration for Others)	29.00	18.59	5.80	11.62	3.97	6.97	4.99	.001
	Relative Morality	31.00	22.82	5.64	16.17	5.52	6.65	4.14	.001
	Conformity	12.00	10.14	4.62	7.66	3.43	2.48	2.16	.05
	Present Time	28.00	19.46	5.25	14.86	6.15	4.59	2.76	.01

TABLE 4.9 A COMPARISON OF THE PRINCIPAL, TEACHERS, AND PARENTS IN JAMES ELEMENTARY SCHOOL (WEIGHTED SCORE MEANS)

	Values	Principal	Teachers (n = 23)		Parents (n = 27)		$Mean_1 - Mean_2$	t	Probability $\leq$
			$Mean_1$	St. Dev.	$Mean_2$	St. Dev.			
Traditional	Work-Success (and Achievement Orientation)	6.00	9.09	6.31	16.59	6.84	−7.51	3.93	.001
	Puritan Morality	4.00	8.04	5.24	16.82	5.37	−8.77	5.40	.001
	Individualism	10.00	14.87	5.15	18.22	4.25	−3.35	2.47	.05
	Future Time	11.00	10.00	4.76	17.37	4.85	−7.27	5.29	.001
Emergent	Sociability (and Consideration for Others)	17.00	19.70	7.90	11.70	3.60	7.99	4.62	.001
	Relative Morality	32.00	24.96	6.48	15.56	4.56	9.40	5.88	.001
	Conformity	14.00	11.04	9.03	5.85	3.68	5.19	2.68	.01
	Present Time	21.00	19.17	7.83	12.33	5.76	6.84	3.52	.01

are usually well educated. The second faction is made up of matriarchal families. These families are less educated, and they have many children. None of the parents take much interest in school. I think that, because they are continually moving, they tend to be less interested in school. There is definitely a value conflict between the parents and the school. The parents want academic training, and the teachers want social training. Social training, however, is not measurable."

"There is no real value difference between the parents and the teachers. However, this community is a low socioeconomic one. Thus, parents work very hard and are too tired to take more of an interest in the school. Both the parents and the teachers want the children to achieve and improve their lives."

"There is no value difference between the parents and the teachers. In fact, parents look up to teachers."

Woodacres It will be recalled that there was a great deal of conflict between school and community over Woodacres' attempt to introduce innovative procedures. The Differential Values Inventory indicated that teachers and parents had significantly different means on five of the value dimensions (Table 4.10). Parents scored significantly higher on three of the traditional values, and for the value of Puritan Morality they also scored higher though not significantly so. Teachers' scores were higher for all emergent dimensions with significant differences for Sociability and Relative Morality. The interviews did support these results, for both the principal and teachers perceived parents as having different values than the faculty. The principal remarked, "I believe that most of the faculty and myself have emergent values. The parents have traditional values. Even though we get a great deal of pressure from many parents, they are not preventing the school from achieving its goals." Some typical comments from teachers are: "The parents do have different values. They do not really care; maybe it is because of their limited education"; and, "Most of the parents that I talk to can be convinced that my ideas are the right ones, but then, after leaving the school, they return to their traditional ways."

Low Organizational Renewal Schools

Fairfield The DVI indicated that teachers and parents had significantly different means on four of the value dimensions (Table 4.11). The only divergence from the Spindler continuum was the traditional

TABLE 4.10 A COMPARISON OF THE PRINCIPAL, TEACHERS, AND PARENTS IN WOODACRES ELEMENTARY SCHOOL (WEIGHTED SCORE MEANS)

	Values	Principal	Teachers (n = 25)		Parents (n = 30)		$Mean_1 - Mean_2$	t	Probability $\leq$
			$Mean_1$	St. Dev.	$Mean_2$	St. Dev.			
Traditional	Work-Success (and Achievement Orientation)	6.00	11.00	6.29	14.63	5.95	−3.63	2.16	.05
	Puritan Morality	10.00	9.44	4.56	11.83	5.00	−2.39	1.80	—
	Individualism	12.00	16.04	2.89	18.33	4.45	−2.29	2.17	.05
	Future Time	8.00	11.52	5.15	14.50	5.20	−2.98	2.09	.05
Emergent	Sociability (and Consideration for Others)	23.00	17.80	4.77	12.63	5.40	5.17	3.66	.001
	Relative Morality	21.00	22.08	5.63	18.03	4.75	4.05	2.84	.01
	Conformity	15.00	7.60	4.09	6.33	3.23	1.27	1.26	—
	Present Time	26.00	15.68	5.15	14.63	5.44	1.05	0.72	—

Individualism dimension where teachers scored very slightly higher than parents. Otherwise, the parents were significantly higher on the other three traditional values and teachers' scores were significantly higher on Relative Morality and tended to be higher though not significantly so on the other emergent dimensions. In this connection, however, it will be recalled from Chapter 3 that the faculty was split along "traditionalist–progressive" lines, with about seventy-five percent of the faculty in the so-called "traditionalist" camp. In the interviews, teachers indicated that parents were not as future-time oriented as themselves, nor were parents as firm in their concepts of right and wrong, though the objective data had revealed the reverse to be true. The following are representative statements made by the faculty:

"Many people in the community are on welfare. Many have only a little education. It is very difficult to get parents to participate. There are several reasons for their lack of participation in school matters: (1) They have an inferiority complex because of having no education; (2) some are very lazy; and (3) some do not speak English. This community is present-time oriented, and the faculty is future-time oriented. If this community is going to be improved, the following will have to be done: (1) The parents must learn English and teach their children English; (2) they must teach their children the difference between right and wrong; i.e., not to fight, steal, or use foul language."

"The parents speak Spanish in the home to preserve their culture. They are torn between the easy life of Mexico and the fast life here. The parents in this community live from day to day; they do not worry about the future."

The teachers' low opinion of their community's minority population can be clearly seen.

Independence The DVI indicated that teachers and parents had significantly different means on all value dimensions except Relative Morality (see Table 4.12). All differences were in the predicted direction. Though interviews partly supported these results, there were a number of teachers who did not perceive a value difference between parents and faculty. Some typical remarks made by teachers were:

"The average family is not concerned with school; they let teachers take care of everything. Fifty percent of the parents are apathetic toward school. The parents want reading to be taught in school, and they do care about their children."

"There is no difference in the values of the parents and those of the teachers."

TABLE 4.11 A COMPARISON OF THE PRINCIPAL, TEACHERS, AND PARENTS IN FAIRFIELD ELEMENTARY SCHOOL (WEIGHTED SCORE MEANS)

Values		Principal	Teachers (n = 38)		Parents (n = 26)		$Mean_1 - Mean_2$	t	Probability $\leq$
			$Mean_1$	St. Dev.	$Mean_2$	St. Dev.			
Traditional	Work-Success (and Achievement Orientation)	5.00	12.29	4.73	15.12	4.40	−2.82	2.38	.05
	Puritan Morality	10.00	10.82	4.51	16.38	5.80	−5.57	4.24	.001
	Individualism	11.00	16.40	3.93	15.42	3.15	0.97	1.04	—
	Future Time	3.00	12.00	6.08	19.00	4.79	−7.00	4.84	.001
Emergent	Sociability (and Consideration for Others)	28.00	16.97	5.29	11.31	3.51	5.67	1.72	—
	Relative Morality	22.00	20.66	5.72	14.58	3.71	6.08	4.70	.001
	Conformity	9.00	9.45	4.18	7.88	4.26	1.56	1.43	—
	Present Time	24.00	15.95	5.90	13.23	4.78	2.72	1.92	—

TABLE 4.12 A COMPARISON OF THE PRINCIPAL, TEACHERS, AND PARENTS IN INDEPENDENCE ELEMENTARY SCHOOL (WEIGHTED SCORE MEANS)

	Values	Principal	Teachers (n = 27)		Parents (n = 28)		$Mean_1 - Mean_2$	t	Probability $\leq$
			$Mean_1$	St. Dev.	$Mean_2$	St. Dev.			
Traditional	Work-Success (and Achievement Orientation)	4.00	10.33	6.40	14.29	6.60	−3.95	2.21	.05
	Puritan Morality	3.00	9.63	5.27	13.82	4.75	−4.19	3.04	.01
	Individualism	16.00	15.56	4.66	18.11	4.48	−2.55	2.03	.05
	Future Time	4.00	10.26	5.04	15.71	6.60	−5.46	3.37	.01
Emergent	Sociability (and Consideration for Others)	31.00	19.44	5.56	12.71	5.48	6.73	4.44	.001
	Relative Morality	32.00	21.37	6.13	18.29	7.02	3.08	1.70	—
	Conformity	10.00	11.63	4.69	8.21	4.49	3.42	2.71	.01
	Present Time	26.00	18.85	5.88	13.89	5.32	4.96	3.22	.01

"I do not think there is a value difference between the faculty and the parents. Both the parents and the teachers want what is best for children."

Bell Street The DVI indicated that teachers and parents had significantly different means on six of the value dimensions (Table 4.13). Only Individualism and Conformity did not reveal significant differences, though again parents scored higher on all traditional dimensions and teachers scored higher on all emergent dimensions. When teachers were interviewed, however, the differences seemed less great than those revealed by statistical analysis.

"Both parents and teachers want what is best for children. Parents are more future-time oriented than teachers, especially in black families."
"There is no real value difference between parents and teachers. However, parents have a more rigid concept of right and wrong."

Mar Villa Mar Villa also fit the expectations of the Spindler continuum, though significant differences were found only on four dimensions: Puritan Morality, Future-Time Orientation, Sociability, and Relative Morality (see Table 4.14). Though the interviews did support that there were value differences, some teachers indicated that parents had less traditional values than the faculty. The objective data had indicated that the opposite was true.

The principal commented, "I think that from fifteen to twenty percent of the parents feel differently about life than do teachers." Typical teacher comments were, "The parents have different values than teachers. The families are split; there are single mothers trying to maintain their families with illegitimate children. The children do not get proper nutrition. Some children are too disciplined; others are not disciplined enough. The only outstanding point about these parents is that they do love their children"; and "The higher socioeconomic families are closer in their values to those of the teachers. The lower socioeconomic families have a harder time appreciating the fine arts, but the families are still ambitious. The parents do come for conferences."

CONCLUSIONS AND RECOMMENDATIONS

In this study teachers were shown to have more traditional values than principals, though they had more emergent values than parents. This finding does not support Spindler's traditional and emergent con-

TABLE 4.13 A COMPARISON OF THE PRINCIPAL, TEACHERS, AND PARENTS IN BELL STREET ELEMENTARY SCHOOL (WEIGHTED SCORE MEANS)

	Values	Principal	Teachers (n = 18)		Parents (n = 24)		$Mean_1 - Mean_2$	t	Probability $\leq$
			$Mean_1$	St. Dev.	$Mean_2$	St. Dev.			
Traditional	Work-Success (and Achievement Orientation)	9.00	11.06	5.55	15.88	7.15	−4.82	2.56	.05
	Puritan Morality	8.00	7.28	4.04	17.58	4.55	−10.30	7.44	.001
	Individualism	9.00	14.94	4.38	17.17	4.03	−2.22	1.65	—
	Future Time	16.00	10.06	5.73	19.38	5.84	−9.32	5.04	.001
Emergent	Sociability (and Consideration for Others)	19.00	18.67	3.85	10.50	4.31	8.17	6.20	.001
	Relative Morality	25.00	22.89	4.47	15.58	5.62	7.31	4.43	.001
	Conformity	8.00	8.44	4.73	6.42	3.35	2.03	1.59	—
	Present Time	26.00	17.28	4.59	12.38	5.73	4.90	2.91	.01

TABLE 4.14 A COMPARISON OF THE PRINCIPAL, TEACHERS, AND PARENTS IN MAR VILLA ELEMENTARY SCHOOL (WEIGHTED SCORE MEANS)

	Values	Principal	Teachers (n = 21)		Parents (n = 25)		$Mean_1 - Mean_2$	t	Probability $\leq$
			$Mean_1$	St. Dev.	$Mean_2$	St. Dev.			
Traditional	Work-Success (and Achievement Orientation)	6.00	10.67	4.45	13.04	5.95	−2.37	1.47	—
	Puritan Morality	7.00	10.00	4.98	14.64	5.20	−4.64	3.01	.01
	Individualism	10.00	16.33	3.89	18.16	4.03	−1.83	1.52	—
	Future Time	4.00	11.24	6.00	17.16	7.34	−5.92	2.90	.01
Emergent	Sociability (and Consideration for Others)	29.00	17.33	5.89	12.56	4.06	4.77	3.16	.01
	Relative Morality	26.00	21.62	5.23	17.96	5.14	3.66	2.33	.05
	Conformity	15.00	9.29	3.73	7.76	4.59	1.53	1.20	—
	Present Time	20.00	16.14	4.35	14.84	6.16	1.30	0.80	—

tinuum in which he assumed that teachers would be less traditional than principals.

Even though statistical significance is not claimed for a comparison of the score of a single principal with the mean score of his staff, an examination of Tables 4.7 to 4.14 indicates that each principal is, on the whole, less traditional and more emergent than his staff. On the traditional dimension Work-Success, each principal in the sample scored lower than the mean score of his teachers. For Puritan Morality and Individualism, six of the eight principals in the sample were less traditional than the teachers in the school. Five of the principals scored lower than their teachers on Future-Time Orientation.

Each principal in the sample was more emergent than his teachers on the Present-Time Orientation dimension. Seven of the eight scored higher than their teachers on the emergent dimensions Sociability and Relative Morality, and five of the eight were more emergent than their teachers on the Conformity dimension. It will be recalled that when the mean scores of all the principals were compared with the mean scores of all the teachers, the principals scored significantly higher on all four emergent dimensions. Teachers scored significantly higher on the traditional dimension Work-Success and Individualism and higher though not significantly so on the other two traditional dimensions.

One explanation of why principals in this study were shown to have more emergent values than teachers may be that the sample schools were all members of the |I|D|E|A| League of Cooperating Schools. League principals had undergone leadership training which encouraged them to allow teachers to experiment with new programs in their classrooms and to decide on the exact goals of the school. For example, some principals felt more comfortable allowing teachers to set their own goals and participated as a member of the group rather than as the leader who directed the group. Therefore, the high scores of the League principals on the two emergent dimensions of Sociability and Relative Morality were not surprising.

Parents' lower scores on the emergent dimensions were not surprising either. Sociability and relative morality are values indicative of individuals who work together in groups in order to attain goals. The League schools encouraged individuals to feel comfortable working together in groups. The socialization process was indeed significant. It may be that the vast majority of parents did not work in any organization that required group action as was found in the League schools, although specific data regarding these kinds of experience was not collected.

How much of the difference in scores between parents and educators occurred because of their respective roles cannot be stated with any certainty. Parents scored very high on the traditional dimensions of Work-Success and Future-Time Orientation; principals and teachers scored significantly lower on these value dimensions. However, parents were responding to these items on the Differential Values Inventory from the role of a parent. Thus, they may have responded from the perspective that, if their children worked hard now and deprived themselves of present enjoyment, they would be more successful in the future. Teachers and principals may have responded to those same items on the Differential Values Inventory not as parents but as members of an organization. Therefore, perhaps depriving oneself of enjoyment in the present and working hard to attain success seemed much less important for teachers and principals. If, on the other hand, they had answered the items which made up the categories of Work-Success and Future-Time Orientation as parents, they might have scored differently on these traditional dimensions. Thus, the differences in values suggested by the scores on the DVI between educators and parents may have resulted from the different roles of the study's respondents.

Spindler assumed that older teachers would be more traditional than younger teachers. This study found no correlation between age and values. For example, though Fairfield and Woodacres both had values which were more traditional than the total sample of teachers' values, Fairfield had the oldest teaching staff of the sample, while Woodacres had the youngest staff. However, most Woodacres teachers lived in or near their school's community, and thus their values may be more reflective of their community than simply reflections of their age.

Since the high OR schools as well as the low OR schools had significant differences in values between parents and educators and between teachers and principals, there seems to be no direct relationship between a lack of congruency in values and the organizational renewal ranking of the school.

Because teachers were stating that they had more contact with parents than parents indicated they had contact with teachers, it appeared that educators were reaching only a small segment of their school communities. In other words, teachers in an individual school may, on the average, have made twenty telephone calls to parents over a period of a year, but some of these parents were called more than once. Thus, the teachers did not, on the average, call twenty different parents. Therefore, teachers were overestimating the number of contacts they had with their school communities.

As a result of this study, we can state that in order to facilitate more effective communication between educators and parents, both should have an awareness and an understanding of each other's values. Knowing the values of their school community helps teachers prevent erroneous assumptions about the community based on commonly held preconceptions. In this study, many teachers perceived their schools' parents inaccurately because they had stereotyped them into an unflattering image. In Fairfield and Mar Villa, some teachers viewed the parents in their schools' communities as having emergent values; i.e., as having a relative sense of morality and being present-time oriented. A large percentage of the families in Fairfield's community was Spanish-speaking, and the teachers felt that these families were not as hard working and future-time oriented as the teachers in the school. However, the results from the Differential Values Inventory showed just the reverse to be true. The parents had more of a traditional set of values than did the teachers. But, because of their conclusions about the parents' values, teachers in Fairfield expected certain types of behavior from parents, and when children were late to school, or even absent from class, some teachers interpreted this as meaning that these families did not respect education.

In other schools, teachers and principals felt that lower socioeconomic families had emergent values, and middle-class or high socioeconomic families had traditional values. As in the Fairfield example above, many teachers and principals confused the behavior of some parents with their values. Teachers failed to realize that many parents probably evaluated their own behavior with a set of traditional values. Some parents might have condemned themselves because they were not successful in their work or because their futures looked bleak. Teachers did not understand that people's behavior is not merely the result of their values but is, in large part, the result of factors acting upon them which originate in their physical and social environments.

On the other hand, if parents understand teachers' values, there exists more chance for them to identify with schools. Parents must feel that schools are providing programs which have taken into account the values of their families. However, since most parents do not have the time to be actively involved with their school, uncertainty arises as to just what purpose the school's programs have. By having the school communicate to parents the values they are trying to instill in their students, confidence in the school can be maintained.

Woodacres was a good example of a school where the community felt that educators had values which were in opposition to theirs. Because several families had complained vociferously about the types of innovative programs in the school, even to the point of writing letters to the community's newspaper, parents throughout the community were beginning to lose confidence in the school. Yet, from the results of the Differential Values Inventory, both teachers and parents were shown to have traditional values. Through the interviews, teachers indicated to the researcher that they wanted the same for their students as parents wanted. If the school had attempted to communicate those values in which it believed, public confidence in the school could have been restored.

There was definitely a communication gap between school and community. Although teachers, especially in these eight elementary schools, spent a significant amount of time contacting parents about their children through telephone calls, letters, and personal visits, they were not reaching the total school community. Instead, teachers were reaching a small segment of the total number of families, perhaps those families whose children were having problems in school. Recognizing that this gap existed, teachers and parents in each school should have attempted to establish and maintain channels of communication appropriate for the particular situation.

As a result of this study of schools which were encouraged to be innovative, we feel that in order for schools to attempt to innovate or change, the administrator's values should be at least as emergent as those of his teaching staff. When an emergent teaching staff wishes to institute change, the principal must allow them to participate in setting goals for the school and in carrying them out. At times, therefore, it is desirable for the administrator to play the role of group member rather than that of group leader. Principals can still help teachers establish goals for new programs even when acting as one member of the group. Individuals with values such as sociability and a flexible standard of morality tend to do well in this type of situation. Because they believe that they should be part of a frictionless group, that right and wrong are defined by the group, and that conformity is, in many instances, advantageous, these individuals work well in activities that require group action.

However, if the principal assumes this role in schools where the teaching staff has a more traditional set of values than he does, a leadership vacuum may develop. In Fairfield, Mar Villa, and Woodacres, which had teachers with the most traditional values, the interviews indicated that, at times, they wanted their principal to be a much stronger leader. Here it would have been to the school's advantage for the principal to balance his behavior between the role of group leader and group member.

NOTES

1   For background materials on the nomothetic and idiographic dimensions, see footnotes 3 and 4 to Chapter 1.
2   Jacob W. Getzels, James M. Lipham, Roald F. Campbell, *Educational Administration as a Social Process,* Harper and Row, New York, 1968, p. 92.
3   George D. Spindler, "Education in a Transforming American Culture," *Harvard Educational Review,* vol. 25, Summer 1955, p. 149. Copyright 1955 by President and Fellows of Harvard College.
4   Ibid., p. 149.
5   Ibid., p. 151.
6   Ibid., p. 150.
7   Richard Prince, "A Study of the Relationships Between Individual Values, Educational Viewpoint, and Local School Approval," unpublished doctoral dissertation, University of Chicago, 1957.

CHAPTER 5

THE SCHOOL
AS A SOCIAL SYSTEM

The Getzels-Guba social systems model has served as the research paradigm for a large number of studies examining the organizational dynamics of schools and related institutions. Typically these studies have selected one dimension of the model, identified tentative hypotheses suggested by the framework, and examined whether such hypotheses are tenable.

The three studies reported in Chapters 2, 3, and 4 of this book fall into this research tradition. Each study selected a dimension of the model (leadership, role–personality conflict, or value orientation) and examined the relationship between that dimension and the school's organizational renewal ranking. The three studies reported herein differed significantly, however, from other one-dimensional efforts, since the data collected came from the same eight schools, each of which was striving to accomplish the same organizational goals for the same period of time. These commonalities provided an opportunity to probe more deeply into the social systems of schools than is possible when unidimensional data are collected from schools striving for different goals, in disparate locations, during different periods of time.

The data collected in these studies enabled the researchers to examine the dynamic interactions among the various components of the social systems model, an important and often neglected dimension in social systems research. Organizations are dynamic, not static. The various components of organizations interact with one another in complex ways within an historical perspective. Any research study of the social system of an organization that does not attempt to examine this dynamic interplay, and account for the historical dimensions as well, misses the very substance of organizational behavior. Accordingly, the researchers' ability to predict or explain organizational behavior is diminished.

The purpose of this chapter is to present an integration of the three dimensions in the sampled elementary schools. The Getzels-Guba model provides the blueprint for the examination of the expected interactions and the effect of the interactions on the schools' ability to achieve a high level of organizational renewal.

The data on which this synthesis is based were reported in Chapters 2, 3, and 4. Here we will be using additional data as well and will depart somewhat from the limitations of the empirical base that characterized the previous discussions. Several years have passed since the schools first formed the League of Cooperating Schools. During those years a number of events occurred that influenced the development of the schools. These events occurred both prior to and since the data collection. We will reflect and attempt to interpret the impact of these events, since to ignore this historical context is to limit severely the interpretation of the research.

In addition, we will attempt to integrate into the synthesis the findings of other research studies that have been conducted in the League Schools. We have examined these studies, discussed them with the appropriate researchers, and sought their reactions to our interpretations of the data we collected and events that we observed. Thus the empirical data presented in Chapters 2, 3, and 4 can be synthesized and interpreted as they fit into a larger picture painted from data of other studies, from the considered judgments of other researchers, and from the historical context within which the schools exist.

This blending of reasonably "hard" empirical data with the "softer" less "rigorous" data adds an ingredient of subjectivity that perhaps some would prefer to avoid. While we are sympathetic to this concern, we feel what is gained from including these data adds significantly to the more comprehensive, integrative approach and more than compensates for the resultant subjectivity.

The format for this synthesis will be the individual case study. The school's comparative ranking on the leader behavior and role–personality conflict dimensions will be discussed, and the data will be interpreted within the broader context of what we have learned about the school from our own observations and from discussions with other researchers.

A special note should be made of the fact that much of the following discussion does not include the value dimension, which was the component of the model examined in Chapter 4. This is because, in the schools studied, there did not appear to be any relationship between the value congruency of the school staff and the community on the one hand, and the schools' organizational renewal ranking on the other. In only one school could the value dimension be seen as indirectly influencing the school's progress. A discussion of the value dimension and its relationship to organizational renewal will appear, however, in the concluding section of this chapter.

Table 5.1 presents graphically what would be expected to result if the theoretical formulations of the Getzels-Guba model are correct.

The categories high, medium high, medium low, and low on congruency of perceived real and ideal leader behavior were determined by rank ordering the schools from personal to normative style. The eight schools were then divided into quartiles: The top two schools were considered high personal style, the next two medium high personal style, the next two medium low, and the bottom two low.

The categories low, medium low, medium high, and high on role–personality conflict were determined by the same method used in determining categories in leader behavior, i.e., ranked from low conflict to high conflict schools. The top two schools were considered low conflict, the next two were designated medium low conflict, the next two medium high conflict, and the last two were high conflict.

An explanation of the way in which the categories crusading, retreatist, ritualist, and insurgent were determined appears in Chapter 3.

TABLE 5.1   EXPECTED CHARACTERISTICS OF HIGH AND LOW OR SCHOOLS

Schools	Perceived leader behavior		Teacher behavior	
	Style	Congruence real–ideal	Role–personality conflict	Conflict adaptation
High Organizational Renewal Schools	Personal	High to Medium High	Low to Medium Low	Crusading
Low Organizational Renewal Schools	Normative	Low to Medium Low	High to Medium High	Insurgent Retreatist Ritualist

Our original hypothesis was that schools that have achieved a high level of organizational renewal would be characterized by the following: (1) They would have a leader who is perceived as having a personal style and would rank high on personal style leader behavior when compared to low OR schools; (2) they would have a low level of teacher role–personality conflict and would rank low on role–personality conflict when compared with low OR schools; and (3) the school's mode of conflict adaptation would more likely be crusading rather than insurgent, retreatist, or ritualist.

Table 5.2 displays how each of the schools compared on the dimensions presented in Table 5.1. In those instances in which the schools met the hypothesized conditions, the appropriate "block" has been left unshaded. Conversely, when the "block" is shaded, the expected conditions in the school were not met. If the research expecta-

TABLE 5.2 SUMMARY OF RESULTS BY SCHOOL

OR	School	Orientation	Congruence real–ideal	Teacher role conflict	Adaptation
High	Seastar	Personal	High (1)*	Low (7)	Crusading
	Shadyside	Personal	Medium (4) High	Low (8)	Crusading
	James	Personal	Low (7)	Medium (5) Low	Insurgent
	Woodacres	Personal	High (2)	Medium (4) High	Crusading
Low	Fairfield	Normative	Medium (6) Low	High (2)	Retreatist
	Independence	Personal	Medium (3) High	Medium (6) Low	Ritualist
	Bell Street	Normative	Medium (5) Low	High (1)	Insurgent
	Mar Villa	Normative	Low (8)	Medium (3) High	Ritualist

▢ = expectations realized
▨ = expectations not realized
* Number indicates the position of the school when the eight sample schools were ranked from highest to lowest.

tions had been met in each instance, the entire chart would be unshaded. The following schools met all of the theoretical expectations: Seastar, Shadyside, Fairfield, Bell Street, and Mar Villa. Woodacres met three of the four expectations, James met two of the expectations, and Independence one.

In the case studies that follow, reference will be made to the data presented in Table 5.2. These data will then be interpreted as they compare with or are explained by additional data from other studies and/or an historical perspective.

HIGH ORGANIZATIONAL RENEWAL SCHOOLS

Seastar

As can be seen from Table 5.2, Seastar meets all of the expectations of the theoretical model. Indeed, it might well be considered a prototype of the model. Data from this study and other |I|D|E|A| studies consistently identify Seastar as achieving the highest level of organizational renewal. Consistent with that condition, Seastar's principal displays personal style leader behavior, though it should be noted that he is not the highest personal style leader in the sample.

The school underwent an interesting and encouraging transformation because of its League participation. When the League of Cooperating Schools was formed, the principal was described as having normative style behavior. Soon after the school's initial participation in the League, the principal became convinced of the value of participative management. He moved to a decidedly personal style, encouraging the faculty to develop its own leadership potential. When a strong teacher leadership emerged, however, the school began to become almost overburdened with faculty proposals for new programs. Gradually the principal saw the need to reassert some leadership in an attempt to coordinate and focus the teachers' efforts. He still used a personal style, but he exerted a somewhat normative leadership style when he felt it was needed. What was occurring in the Seastar principal's behavior was the gradual emergence of what Getzels refers to as the transactional style of leadership, i e, "the need for moving toward one style under one set of circumstances and toward the other style under another set of circumstances."[1] Apparently, he was successful in convincing his teachers of the appropriateness of his leader behavior, for the school had the highest congruency between the teachers' perception of real and ideal leader behavior of all of the eight sample schools. There were no significant differences between real and ideal principal leader behavior on any of the twelve dimensions of the LBDQ-XII. In fact, Seastar showed the least real and ideal expectational differences of the eight sample schools on seven of the twelve leader behavior dimensions. Seastar was also the second lowest of the eight schools in terms of role–personality conflict, thus indicating high congruency between principal and teacher perceptions of each other's roles. The faculty had assumed a crusading mode of adaptation. Obviously they believed in the goals and values of the school and felt that through their efforts they could effect changes they thought were important.

Seastar appears to have achieved a careful balance between the principal's behavior and the teachers' expectations of leader behavior, and this resulted in a high level of attainment in organizational renewal.

Shadyside

Shadyside also fits the theoretical expectations of the model. The principal was the highest personal style leader in the sample, though, as will be noted below, this personal style proved to be somewhat dysfunctional in this school in the years that followed the data collection. Shadyside ranks medium high in the congruence between real and ideal leader behavior. The level of role–personality conflict is low, and the school faculty can be characterized as having adopted a crusading mode of adaptation.

When viewed in an historical perspective, unfortunately, Shadyside's level of success proved to be short lived. When Shadyside originally entered the League of Cooperating Schools, it was led by a strong, resourceful principal who funneled the faculty's energies and talents into the development of a sound, innovative instructional program. He was the driving force in implementing organizational renewal and initiating significant changes in the school. In so doing, the principal developed a strong and independent faculty leadership similar to that found in Seastar.

At the beginning of the year in which these data were collected, a new principal took over. He was a personal style leader and non-directive, hence the school was able to capitalize on the strong faculty leadership that had developed under the former principal and the school continued to prosper. One might reasonably expect this condition would have continued indefinitely had there been no substantial alteration of the principal and staff composition. Unexpectedly, a significant shift did occur. The school district in which Shadyside was located underwent a court-ordered program of racial integration. As a means of meeting the court's integration guidelines, school faculties were shuffled. The former K–6 elementary schools were designated either K–3 or 4–6. Thus between two previously K–6 schools, all the K–3 teachers were assigned to one school, and all the 4–6 teachers were assigned to the other school. Shadyside was designated a K–3 school. As a result of this realignment, the faculty cohesion was broken. The leadership style of the past was unfamiliar to the new teachers. Fully one-half of the staff was unacquainted with the "participative" management that had characterized the school in the recent few years; the newly arrived faculty was used to a more traditional approach.

What clearly was needed was a shift in leader behavior to a more normative style in order to build faculty leadership once again. Unfortunately the principal persisted with the nondirective participative approach which had been successful with the former faculty. The result, one year after the data collection, was a leadership vacuum. The staff was looking to the principal for leadership, and he was expecting the faculty to provide it, as it had in the recent past. The school was struggling to recapture the spirit and thrust it formerly enjoyed.

James

The reader will note from Table 5.2 that James deviates somewhat from the theoretical expectations. The principal has a personal style, but there is a low congruency between the real and ideal leader behavior orientation. Although there is medium low teacher–role conflict, the faculty is characterized by an insurgent mode of adaptation.

We believe this inconsistency can be explained by events that took place before and during the questionnaire phase of data collection. The principal and teachers had built a strong school around mutual trust and congruency of appropriate leader behavior. However, just prior to our data collection, the school underwent the agonies of a threatened districtwide teacher strike. Many of the teachers in the school were prepared to follow union strike directives, and, for reasons discussed in Chapter 3, the principal was deeply hurt by these intentions. In response, he became very normative in his actions, and the faculty reacted by questioning the appropriateness of his behavior.

Considerable turmoil resulted, and this is reflected in the low congruency between real and ideal behavior and the insurgent mode of adaptation as evidenced in the questionnaire data. The interviews two months later revealed that though the strike bitterness was not forgotten entirely, the situation had reverted to its former harmonious relationship.

This conflict between the principal and teachers at James School illustrates what is likely to be a common occurrence in American public schools as teachers adopt a more militant stance and move increasingly to a collective bargaining model to achieve what they believe is in the best interests of teachers and schools. In the past, many elementary principals have tended to think of the teachers as "their teachers" and of the school as "one big happy family." However, the collective negotiations model assumes a fundamental conflict between labor (teachers) and management (principals), as opposed to the more cooperative stance that had characterized the principal–teacher relationship in the past. This shift from a cooperative to a conflict relationship may require a reexamination of some parts of the Getzels-Guba model.[2]

What is meant by this is that the Getzels model was developed at a time when a basic problem of elementary school leadership was to resolve conflicts that were essentially internal in origin. For example, employees may have differed over the desirability of certain actions of the leader or of selected organizational practices or requirements. The major solution to these conflicts could be found within the organization, as ways were sought to achieve a greater congruency between the employee's personal needs and dispositions and the practices and demands of the organization. The kinds of problems found in the schools tended to differ from school to school and depended largely on the mix of individuals who comprised the organization and the setting in which the organization existed. One could, of course, make some generalizations about the classification of conflicts one might find (e.g., allocation of space, handling discipline problems, personality conflicts). Nonetheless the specific problems found differed from school to school, and they were generally amenable to the specific action that principals might take to alleviate them.

With the introduction of collective bargaining however, a change occurs in the nature of problems found in the school and the extent to which they can be expected to respond to the principal's corrective actions. A far greater number of conflicts are brought into the school from the external environment. That is the teachers' organization or union establishes minimum conditions it feels are essential to the teachers' welfare. These concerns often result in a set of common conflicts in several schools at the same time, and these conflicts are generated from a source external to the school. We do not examine whether this development is beneficial or not, we merely wish to point out one result of this development, namely, that much of the conflict in the school has a source that is external to the school.

Another result, and perhaps a more important one, is that a common effect of moving to a collective bargaining model is that the concept of an unresolvable conflict between labor (teachers) and management (administration) is internalized in teachers and administrators. The basic trust necessary in the search for congruency between organizational and personal needs can be seriously eroded.

Both of these developments—the introduction of general problems and conflicts into the school from *external* sources and the assumption of a basic conflict between teachers and administrators—require that the Getzels model be expanded or more broadly interpreted. No longer can the local school be viewed as the only entity that has influence and power to resolve these conflicts.

Woodacres

Woodacres meets three of the four theoretical expectations. The principal has a personal style, there is high congruency between real and ideal leadership expectations, the faculty has a crusading mode of adaptation. The level of role–personality conflict, however, is medium high.

We believe that the conflict is a result of the faculty's having to respond to divergent and often conflicting pressures on the school, largely from external sources. This school, more than any of the other seven in the sample, has encountered considerable community resistance. The school has the newest and most obviously experimental architectural plan; thus, the "experimental" nature of the school is readily apparent to the most casual observer. While the school district is decidedly middle class, Woodacres' student population is from the lower socioeconomic end of the district's population. The pupils had the lowest measured reading scores of any school in the district. The juxtaposition of the low reading scores and the experimental program led some parents to assume a direct relationship between the experimental program and low student achievement. As a result, early in the history of the school's participation in the League of Cooperating Schools, considerable public opposition to the school developed. This had a devastating effect on the school. The faculty's confidence in what it was attempting to do was shaken, and there was considerable faculty turnover. They looked for leadership from the principal, but it was not forthcoming.

In the year after the data collection, the school's program appeared to have "taken hold." The reading scores improved markedly, and public disenchantment subsided. The faculty turnover slowed, and the school appeared to have weathered the storm of discontent and to be moving along nicely in achieving its goals. Indeed, when a decision was made recently to transfer the school's principal to another school, many of those teachers who had earlier sought his removal rallied to his support and requested that he remain at the school.

Woodacres is the only school in the sample in which the values orientation of the parents influenced the school's success. The parents valued their children making progress in school. When the reading scores were low, they exerted considerable pressure to alter what they considered a major reason for the school's failure—the experimental educational program. This pressure seriously affected the faculty's confidence in what they were doing, and the high conflict resulted. With the increase of public support for the school, we believe the level of teacher conflict has subsided considerably.

LOW ORGANIZATIONAL RENEWAL SCHOOLS

Fairfield

Fairfield fits the theoretical expectations of a school that has had difficulty in effecting a high level of organizational renewal. The school principal exhibits normative style behavior, there is medium low congruence between real and ideal leader behavior and a high level of role–personality conflict, and the faculty is characterized as retreatist in its mode of adaptation.

The school exhibits several characteristics that we think help explain its present state. The faculty has been at the school for many years, and they differ racially from the school population they serve. The faculty exhibits a lack of confidence in the ability of the pupils to achieve, given the social and economic conditions under which many of the students must live. What is more, they do not possess much confidence in their principal's ability to lead them. The principal talks about participative management, but his actions are not consistent with that style; he has remained very normative. Thus a sort of hopelessness has developed. The faculty has little expectation of seeing significant changes in their leader and lacks the wherewithal to effect a significant change in the school's functioning. The retreatist mode of adaptation aptly describes the school's atmosphere.

Independence

This school exhibited a low OR score, yet it does not conform to the hypothetical expectations of the model. The principal has a personal style, there is medium high congruence on the real–ideal leadership behavior and a medium low level of role–personality conflict, although the school does exhibit a ritualist mode of adaptation.

We believe a look at the history of the school will help explain this inconsistency. During the three years preceding the data collection, the faculty of Independence School was located in two separate buildings that were several miles apart, although they shared the same principal. The data were collected at a time when the faculties had been brought together for only a few months. The physical separation had influenced the organizational renewal ranking negatively because it had been difficult for the two faculties to meet often. Nonetheless, they were led by a personal style principal who conformed to their expectations, and they exhibited little role–personality conflict in implementing the goals to which they were committed. Since the data collection, this school has prospered. Even the desegregation plan imposed by the district did not affect the school's functioning, since the principal was able to alter his behavior to promote faculty leadership among the half of the faculty that were new to the school. We believe that, were this school's level of organizational renewal measured today, it would be very high indeed.

Bell Street

Bell Street School meets the hypothetical expectations for a low OR school, i.e., normative leadership style, medium low real and ideal leader behavior congruency, high role–personality conflict, and an insurgent mode of adaptation.

Bell Street is similar to Fairfield in that it serves a student population that differs in racial composition from its faculty, and its principal is not considered by the faculty to be a particularly effective leader. It differs from Fairfield, however, in that its faculty is younger and has some strong leadership within its ranks. This relatively small cadre of teachers is providing a much needed leadership component. The principal is well liked personally and encourages the teachers to try to change the educational program to meet the students' needs. Recent observations indicate that the school is making progress, although a principal who exhibited what the teachers might consider more effective leader behavior might well increase significantly the tempo of change.

Mar Villa

Mar Villa School's low organizational renewal ranking is consistent with the hypothetical expectations of the model, i.e., normative leader style, low congruence between real and ideal leader behavior, medium high role–personality conflict, and a ritualist mode of role adaptation.

This school is similar to Fairfield in that its leadership is viewed by the faculty as ineffective and its faculty lacks strong internal leadership. It differs in that it does not face the task of educating a student population that differs racially from the faculty. This school is essentially a case of a school that was mandated by superordinates to undergo educational change. Indeed the staff recently moved into a new building that was clearly designed to house an innovative program. But the school does not have a "critical mass" of faculty or administrative leadership talent to bring about the changes. As a result, the school will likely not change significantly until leadership in the form of the principal or a cadre of faculty emerges to set the school on course, although recently there appears to be some movement toward this end.

CONCLUSIONS AND RECOMMENDATIONS

Expectations of the Getzels Model

The relationships that we had predicted between high and low organizational renewal ranking and the conditions in the schools as they re-

lated to the selected dimensions of the Getzels-Guba model proved
to be partially true. An examination of the synthesis of the data collected from the various instruments (presented in Table 5.2) reveals
that the relationship between the leader behavior dimension and the
role–personality conflict dimension met our expectations in the schools
at the extreme ends of the continuum of high to low OR schools (i.e.,
the two highest schools and the two lowest schools). The picture is
not as clear when the results from the middle four schools are examined. We think we have been able to identify from the extended
analyses presented here reasons why the results in these schools were
somewhat mixed. There may be another reason, of course. It is possible that these schools were more similar to one another than the
"extreme schools" in their OR rankings, and our instruments were not
sufficiently refined to pick up the more subtle differences. We are in-
clined to discount this explanation, however, because the eight schools
were selected from the original population of eighteen League schools.
Thus, we have already left out the middle fourteen schools and, therefore, all of the eight schools in this sample are relatively "extreme."

Our expectation that there would be a relationship between the
value dimension and organizational renewal was not realized. We are
not exactly sure as to why this is so. It would be premature to interpret
the findings to mean that the Getzels-Guba model is inappropriate in
considering the value dimension important in the functioning of an
elementary school. This finding would not be consistent with other
research into the value dimension as it relates to schools, nor does it
seem logical that the value dimension would have little influence on
the operation of institutions that are as value-laden as elementary
schools. Indeed, one can point to experiences in many communities
attempting value-laden changes in the schools which have brought
severe repercussions. A good example of this is the controversies that
have developed in some communities over the introduction of sex
education into the curriculum. Some schools have virtually been closed
down and the careers of principals and teachers drastically affected by
hostile community reaction. The same has been true over efforts to
introduce racial integration or teach about Communism.

Our conclusion as regards the lack of differences between high
and low OR schools on value congruency is that the kinds of changes
being implemented in the League schools for some reason were not
such that they touched the value systems of the communities involved.
Whether this was because the schools had carefully built public sup-

port for what they were doing or because the public just did not know or care, we do not know. We hypothesize, however, that if these changes were viewed as value-laden in the communities, the expected relationship between value congruency and OR would have become manifest. It is instructive to us to think of schools as operating in a value force field, so to speak. As long as the activities in the school do not appear to threaten the value system of a significant population of the community, the school is largely left to carry out its responsibilities without interference. If, however, the school activities are inconsistent with the community value system, the protective barrier between school and community is quickly broken, the public forcefully asserts its will, and the school's functioning is dramatically affected.

Collective Bargaining and Future Conflict in Schools

If the Getzels-Guba model is correct as regards the necessity for congruency on such matters as leader behavior, role expectations, and value orientations—and we believe that it is—then we predict that schools will find it more and more difficult to achieve their goals in the years ahead. The reason for this speculation is the increasing use of collective bargaining in education. The collective bargaining model assumes that there is a basic conflict between labor (teachers) and management (school administrators and school boards) and that, while one can try to reduce this conflict, it can never be totally removed because it is inherent in the differing expectations that labor and management have for the allocation of limited resources. This inherent conflict orientation is in contrast to the congruency assumptions of the Getzels model.

In saying this, however, we do not wish to imply that schools in the past have been totally harmonious and happy organizations and that teachers have deliberately chosen to disrupt a previously productive relationship by turning to collective bargaining to achieve their goals. We know that many schools have had a long history of conflict between teachers and administrators, although often such conflicts have been muted because teachers have felt they did not have the right or the power to take the steps necessary to enforce their demands. We know, also, that for some teachers and teacher organizations the decision to use collective bargaining to achieve what they consider to be legitimate goals has been a last resort. Nonetheless, teachers have adopted this strategy, and one can expect that conflicts such as occurred at James School will increasingly reduce the ability of the schools to achieve their goals.

The conflict crisis may be resolved in a number of ways. For example, teachers and administrators and school board members may find that the price paid for achieving goals through the collective bargaining process is too high in terms of disruption and deteriorating working relationships and, therefore, search for more cooperative and productive ways of resolving conflicts. Or the inherent value system of teachers, administrators, and school board members, as related to the need for congruency, may simply change, and they may learn to work together productively with a relatively high level of conflict. Whatever the means of adjustment, we predict it will take time, and until such adjustments are completed, the schools' ability to perform will be significantly hampered.

The Historical Perspective

As a basic recommendation for researchers, we view it as absolutely essential that any study of the social systems of schools consider the historical development of the school. Not to do so may result in serious errors in data interpretation. In this study, for example, merely collecting and analyzing the initial questionnaire data would have led to significant errors in our research conclusions. A school is an accumulation of past events, events that may be hidden from immediate view, yet these occurrences manifest themselves in many subtle and important ways in the research results.

What has been said of the influence of past history as it relates to research methodology is equally true of school district practices as they influence the selection of administrators for schools and the implementation of new programs or practices. Schools differ on important organizational variables, such as level of employee role–personality conflict, expected leader behavior, or value congruency, and decisions regarding the staffing and operation of schools should account for this fact. Yet such variables seldom are considered in making decisions regarding schools, particularly in urban areas. Administrators are often assigned to schools because they are "next on the list," or successful or unsuccessful in another school.

We realize the difficulty in selecting administrators on, say, the basis of the congruency factors suggested in this study. District administrators often have to consider other factors, such as experience of principals, need for a principal to be moved from an "easy" school to a "difficult" one (or vice versa), or the informal structure that influences such decisions. Moreover, it is difficult, perhaps impossible, for central administrators to measure accurately some of these important dimensions, even if they wanted to respond accordingly.

Nonetheless, the point should not be forgotten. The probability of developing efficient and effective schools will likely be low until the congruency on these important variables is maximized. We would point to the example of Shadyside as a school in which lack of attention to these variables severely retarded the school's progress.

A related point is that we were impressed with the amount of time it takes to develop a school into a smoothly functioning organization, particularly when the school is undertaking significant change. Everyone has to adopt new norms and adjust to new ways. This is time consuming and difficult. None of these schools really was functioning very smoothly until at least two years of their League participation had passed; some were just beginning to make progress at the end of four years. Yet some school districts, particularly urban districts, move administrators around frequently as if they were merely neutral components that will fit in equally well in any school. Again, there may be political or social or bureaucratic reasons as to why this is necessary. The point is that any district that has high turnover of administrators in schools cannot expect to have much success in developing smoothly functioning schools or instituting significant changes.

The Leader of the Future

The data generally supported the hypothesis that the personal style leader is congruent with a high level of organizational renewal. However, those leaders whom we regarded as the most successful exhibited a transactional style of behavior; in other words, their leader behavior was consciously shifted from personal style to normative style as conditions changed. It is important to note that these leaders were encouraging the development of an organization in which personal style would be the most common leader behavior required. However, since leadership is a function of followership, a successful leader must have both a repertoire of leader behaviors upon which he can draw and the insight to know when different types of leader behavior are appropriate.

Toward the School of the Future

There is no question in our minds as to the need for change in America's public schools. For all too long the schools have continued to operate under the same general format, based on one set of assumptions. To be sure, there have been many who have worked very hard to introduce change into the schools; however, except for a few notable examples, their efforts have been largely ineffectual. The reason "change agents" have not been very successful in effecting long-range change in schools is not because what they were trying to accomplish was of little value or because they were insincere or gave up too easily, although no doubt these factors have marked some unsuccessful efforts. We believe a fundamental reason for such failures is that change agents have underestimated the complexity of the organization they dealt with. Often they have viewed the problem as mainly that of convincing professionals that some new innovative scheme or program will result in increased learning for pupils. Thus these strategies have included demonstrations of the technique, reporting research results, and conducting in-service sessions. They have assumed that intelligent, interested educators will accept eagerly that which is proven to be better. Sometimes, however, their enthusiasm has blinded them to the complexity of the task. What they have neglected all too often in their strategies has been the structure and dynamic personal interactions, many times informal, that blunt the edge of change efforts.

The research reported here represents an attempt to examine, and thereby illustrate, the complexity of introducing change into elementary schools. We hope that by our exploratory efforts we have made the reader cognizant of some of the dimensions of organizations that must be considered when attempting to effect change. We hope the reader is now more aware of the need to balance various organizational components, such as leaders and followers, so that a positive relationship will result which will, in turn, make progress possible. In addition, we hope the reader is acquainted with the importance of viewing organizations in their historical context and of altering organizational components when demanded by significant changes in external environmental conditions.

Finally, we hope the reader is convinced of the value of using a theoretical base for examining the school's social system. Such systems are very complex, and one can flounder indefinitely in seeking a way to grasp the totality of the system if he is unaided by some blueprint or plan. We found the Getzels-Guba model to be useful for this purpose, although we have utilized only a small portion of that formulation in this exploratory effort.

We hope that our efforts will spur further comprehensive inquiries into the social system of schools and the effect such systems have on innovation. What is more, we hope that our work will forge at least a small linkage between the all-too-separate worlds of theory–research and practice. Only by building such linkages can we hope to build a solid basis upon which to improve the introduction and management of innovations intended to improve the quality of American education.

NOTES

1 Jacob W. Getzels, James M. Lipham, and Roald F. Campbell, *Educational Administration as a Social Process: Theory, Research, Practice,* Harper & Row, New York, 1968, p. 148.

2 Charles R. Perry and Wesley A. Wildman, *The Impact of Negotiations in Public Education: The Evidence from the Schools,* Charles A. Jones, Worthington, Ohio, 1970, pp. 218–219.

SOCIOECONOMIC DESCRIPTION OF THE EIGHT SAMPLE SCHOOLS

Seastar Elementary School

The school is situated in an independently incorporated community located in the western section of a large metropolitan area of Southern California. The school attendance area is almost completely residential with a predominance of single-family dwelling units. Along the eastern boundary of the attendance area there is a new condominium development. On the southeast boundary there is a commercial development.

The children in the regular attendance area are from predominantly white-collar backgrounds. The majority of homes in the area sell for $26,000–$30,000.

There has been a substantial change in the racial composition of the school population since 1960, with Oriental students composing eight to nine percent of the student population. This is an increase from one percent in 1960. There has also been a slight rise in the Mexican-American population. The school attendance figures indicate about five to six percent of the students have Spanish surnames.

Shadyside Elementary School

The school is situated in an independently incorporated community, located in the southwestern section of a large metropolitan area of Southern California. The school is less than a mile northeast of a large international airport. The attendance area includes a commercial area along the main street that runs through the area and a light manufacturing area that is along the western boundary of the attendance area.

The school is located in a community that has two disparate populations: white collar and blue collar. The white-collar and upper blue-collar familes have children that are of high school and college age. Many are retired residents of long duration who moved to the community when it was being subdivided before and just after the Second World War. They supply almost none of the school population.

Also within the school attendance area are two trailer courts where people rent trailers and spaces at a low cost. Nearby, many of the houses have cottages in the rear that are rented for moderate prices. These residences are in various stages of upkeep. The school population comes from these types of housing and tends to be drawn from families of blue-collar backgrounds.

James Elementary School

The school is located in a large city on the southern border of California and is situated in the center of U.S. Military housing for noncommissioned officers. Approximately eighty percent of the school population is drawn from military housing. The other twenty percent are drawn from a tract of homes to the south of the school. Though the school plant is old, the area it serves is fairly new.

Woodacres Elementary School

The school is located northwest of a large metropolitan area of Southern California in a newly built tract of homes that range from $18,000–$25,000 in price. The tract is located on a hillside overlooking the community. All the homes are new and well kept. The attendance area is removed from local manufacturing and commercial areas and is completely residential. The only nonresidential structure in the area is the school itself. The families that populate the school attendance area are uniformly young and have many children.

Fairfield Elementary School

The school is located in a farming community in the southern portion of central California. The community is separated from the eastern section of the city by the Southern Pacific Railroad right-of-way and the packing houses that are adjacent to the tracks. The population of the west community is composed of minority-group members: Mexican-Americans, Negroes, and Filipinos. Housing in the west community ranges from a few clapboard shacks at the southern end to a well-kept housing tract at the northern end. The tract homes are modest, probably within the $12,000–$15,000 range. Sprinkled throughout the area are a few isolated homes that are worth $20,000 or more. All of the streets are paved, and most have sidewalks. There are four or five family-owned corner grocery stores in the area. West of the freeway there is one commercial service center, consisting of a locally owned grocery store and a few small businesses. Between the freeway and the railroad tracks are older, small houses and cottage courts, many of which are in states of deterioration. In this area there is a row of taverns and cheap eating establishments.

The population of the school community consists predominantly of farm workers and various gradations of blue-collar workers.

Independence Elementary School

The school is situated in an independently incorporated community located in a valley northeast of a large metropolitan area of Southern California. The school attendance area is close to the center of the suburb. The homes are quite old, yet well kept. There are some newer structures in the area, but there has been practically no building of single-family dwelling units since 1960. All new building has been apartment houses with three to nine units each.

Since 1960, many homes have been removed from the school attendance area to make room for a new freeway right-of-way. The homes that were removed were occupied primarily by elderly retired people, so even though the homes were removed the school attendance rose slightly.

From all indications, the school is on the verge of a period of rapid transition from a predominantly white-collar to a blue-collar school population.

The following alterations have taken place in the 1960 census indicators: (1) the percentage of people of fifty-five or older has dropped to about twenty-five percent; (2) the percentage of lower blue-collar workers has increased; (3) the percentage of renter-occupied units has risen to sixty percent; (4) single-family dwelling units have dropped about four percent while units with three to nine units have increased; and (5) homes built previous to 1939 have dropped about five percent.

Bell Street Elementary School

The school is situated along the eastern boundary of a coastal community located west of a large metropolitan area in Southern California. The area contains a commercial section, a residential area, and light manufacturing. The housing ranges from small wood frame houses built in the 1920s to modern apartment complexes. The area is dotted with trailer courts, stucco homes, and older apartment houses.

Since the 1960 census data were gathered, a freeway was built through the school attendance area. The construction of the freeway had the following effects: (1) It eliminated nearly all of the upper white-collar workers who resided in the school attendance area. The path of the freeway went through the most expensive houses in the area. (2) It dropped the percent of the Caucasian students attending the school. The upper white-collar workers were predominantly Caucasian with a few Orientals. The Oriental proportion of the school population also dropped as a result of the freeway construction. (3) It dropped the median age of the area. Those people who were relocated as a result of the freeway construction were older and more established, with mature families.

Approximately twenty percent of the school population has been identified as at the poverty level. The percentage of minority-group students has been steadily increasing since 1955. Since then, the school has been receiving greater amounts of students on welfare. Since the freeway was built, an optional attendance area was included in an upper white-collar area adjacent to the school attendance area. No students from the optional area attend the school.

In summary, the attendance area of the school is in transition from predominantly white collar to a predominantly blue collar. Single dwelling units are being removed to provide space for multiple dwelling units.

Mar Villa Elementary School

The school is situated in a large coastal community, located at the northern boundary of Southern California. The school draws its student population from three areas that have vastly different characteristics. Most of the students come from a suburban development that was built in the middle of the 1950s. This area is refered to as "the mesa." The mesa contains a population of predominantly white-collar workers. The homes are well kept and have a resale value of between $17,000–$23,000. The second area that the school draws from is the beach motel area. It is not known exactly how many students attend from this area. The third section is an old section of the beach community located in the southwest portion of the community. This area contains a high predominance of Mexican-American children, intermediate and lower blue-collar workers, and old housing.

Some of the changes since 1960 are: (1) higher incidence of working mothers; (2) dwindling of upper white-collar workers to about fifteen percent; (3) increase in apartment complexes of ten or more units; (4) an increase in deteriorating and dilapidated homes; and (5) an increase in renter-occupied housing. Many of the people moving from the tract on the mesa are not selling their homes, but keeping them and renting.

GLOSSARY

DEFINITION OF TERMS

Principal The individual designated as the official leader of the school.

Teacher A certified individual engaged in the instruction of pupils in grades K through 6.

Community The parents of all students attending an elementary school under study.

STATISTICAL TERMS

Chi-square analysis A statistical test used to determine whether or not two groups differ significantly in respect to some characteristic when the data consist of frequencies in discrete categories. An example of the use of this test may be found in Chapter 3. In order to determine whether or not low OR schools had a greater proportion of teachers with high role–personality conflict scores than high OR schools, teachers were assigned to a two-by-two frequency table on the basis of high or low conflict scores and high or low OR school membership.

Mann-Whitney U A technique for comparing median scores in order to determine whether or not two groups are significantly different in respect to some characteristic. It is appropriate for small samples when the measurement is at least ordinal, but does not require interval scaling.

Null hypothesis A statement to the effect that two groups will not be different in respect to some measurable characteristic. Mean scores, proportions, and correlation coefficients may be compared by appropriate statistical methods in order to determine whether differences between two groups are statistically significant.

Statistical significance A statement to the effect that differences between groups or relationships between variables are greater than would have occurred by chance.

t-test For small samples ($N < 30$) Fisher's t is a statistic used to compare the mean scores for two groups on some variable to determine whether or not any difference that exists between the two groups can be said to be statistically significant. Formula for testing difference between uncorrelated means:

$$t = \frac{M_1 - M_2}{\sqrt{\left(\frac{\Sigma x^2_1 + \Sigma x^2_2}{N_1 + N_2 - 2}\right)\left(\frac{N_1 + N_2}{N_1 N_2}\right)}}$$

Formula for testing difference between correlated means:

$$t = \frac{M_d}{\sqrt{\dfrac{\Sigma x^2_d}{N(N-1)}}}$$

A 2-tail test is used when a null hypothesis is being tested. A 1-tail test is appropriate when a directional hypothesis is being tested, for example, when it is hypothesized that the mean score for Group A will be larger than the mean score for Group B on a given variable.

More detailed information regarding these terms may be found in any comprehensive statistics text, for example: J. P. Guilford, *Fundamental Statistics in Psychology and Education*, McGraw-Hill, New York, 1956; Sidney Siegel, *Nonparametric Statistics for the Behavioral Sciences*, McGraw-Hill, New York, 1956.

INDEX